Contents

W9-BXC-294

i

Contents

Name _____

Strategy Workshop

As you listen to the story "The Pumpkin Runner," by Marsha Diane Arnold, you will stop from time to time to do some activities on these practice pages. These activities will help you think about different strategies that can help you read better. After completing each activity, you will discuss what you've written with your classmates and talk about how to use these strategies.

Remember, strategies can help you become a better reader. Good readers

- use strategies whenever they read

- use different strategies before, during, and after reading

- think about how strategies will help them

Name _____

Strategy 1: Predict/Infer

Use this strategy before and during reading to help make predictions about what happens next or what you're going to learn.

Here's how to use the Predict/Infer strategy:

1. Think about the title, the illustrations, and what you have read so far.
2. Tell what you think will happen next—or what you will learn. Thinking about what you already know about the topic may help.
3. Try to figure out things the author does not say directly.

Listen as your teacher begins "The Pumpkin Runner." When your teacher stops, complete the activity to show that you understand how to predict what you think might happen in the story.

Think about the story and respond to the question below.

What do you think might happen in the story?

_____

_____

_____

_____

As you continue listening to the story, think about whether your prediction was right. You might want to change your prediction or write a new one below.

_____

_____

_____

_____

_____

Name _____

Strategy 2: Phonics/Decoding

Use this strategy during reading when you come across a word you don't know.

Here's how to use the Phonics/Decoding Strategy:

1. Look carefully at the word.
2. Look for word parts that you know and think about the sounds for the letters.
3. Blend the sounds to read the word.
4. Ask yourself if this is a word you know and whether the word makes sense in the sentence.
5. If not, ask yourself what else you can try. Should you look in a dictionary?

Listen as your teacher continues to read the story. When your teacher stops, use the Phonics/Decoding Strategy.

Now write down the steps you used to decode the word *hundred*.

_____

_____

_____

_____

_____

_____

_____

_____

_____

Remember to use this strategy whenever you are reading and come across a word that you don't know.

Name _____

Strategy 3: Monitor/Clarify

Use this strategy during reading whenever you're confused about what you are reading.

Here's how to use the Monitor/Clarify strategy:

- Ask yourself if what you're reading makes sense—or if you are learning what you need to learn.
- If you don't understand something, reread, use the illustrations, or read ahead to see if that helps.

Listen as your teacher continues to read the story. When your teacher stops, complete the activity to show that you understand how to figure out why Joshua talks about his herd when the other contestant talks about training for the race.

Think about the story and respond below.

1. What do you know about Joshua?

_____

_____

_____

_____

2. Can you tell from listening to the story why Joshua talks about checking his herd? Why or why not?

_____

_____

_____

_____

3. How can you find out why Joshua isn't talking about training?

_____

_____

_____

Name _____

Strategy 4: Question

Use this strategy during and after reading to ask questions about important ideas in the story.

Here's how to use the Question strategy:

- Ask yourself questions about important ideas in the story.
- Ask yourself if you can answer these questions.
- If you can't answer the questions, reread and look for answers in the text. Thinking about what you already know and what you've read in the story may help you.

Listen as your teacher continues to read the story. When your teacher stops, complete the activity to show that you understand how to ask yourself questions about important ideas in the story.

Think about the story and respond below.

Write a question you might ask yourself at this point in the story.

_____

_____

_____

_____

_____

_____

_____

_____

_____

If you can't answer your question now, think about it while you listen to the rest of the story.

Name _____

Strategy 5: Evaluate

Use this strategy during and after reading to help you form an opinion about what you read.

Here's how to use the Evaluate strategy:

- Think about how the author makes the story come alive and makes you want to read it.
- Think about what was entertaining, informative, or useful about the selection.
- Think about how you reacted to the story—how well you understood the selection and whether you enjoyed reading it.

Listen as your teacher continues to read the story. When your teacher stops, complete the activity to show that you are thinking of how you feel about what you are reading and why you feel that way.

Think about the story and respond below.

1. Tell whether or not you think this story is entertaining and why.

   _____

   _____

   _____

2. Is the writing clear and easy to understand?

   _____

   _____

   _____

3. This is an adventurous fiction story. Did the author make the characters believable and interesting?

   _____

   _____

Name _____

Strategy 6: Summarize

Use this strategy after reading to summarize what you read.

Here's how to use the Summarize strategy:
- Think about the characters.
- Think about where the story takes place.
- Think about the problem in the story and how the characters solve it.
- Think about what happens in the beginning, middle, and end of the story.

Think about the story you just listened to. Complete the activity to show that you understand how to identify important story parts that will help you summarize the story.

Think about the story and respond to the questions below:

1. Who is the main character?

_____

_____

_____

2. Where does the story take place?

_____

_____

_____

3. What is the problem and how is it resolved?

_____

_____

_____

_____

Now use this information to summarize the story for a partner.

Name _____

Think About Journeys

What kinds of journeys do you know about? Use the space below to jot down all kinds of journeys.

Journeys I've taken	Journeys taken by people I know	Journeys from books, the movies, or TV

Choose one of the journeys above that was really important to the person who took it, and answer the following questions:

Who took the journey?

_____

Where did that person go and why?

_____

_____

How or why was that experience important?

_____

_____

_____

Challenges Along the Way

As you read, complete the chart below for each story.

	What problems or challenges do the characters face on their journey?	Why is the journey important to the characters?
Akiak		
Grandfather's Journey		
Finding the Titanic		
By the Shores of Silver Lake		

Name _____

Cold Words

Match each word to its definition by writing the letter on the line beside the word. Then answer the questions that follow.

____ blizzard

____ checkpoint

____ courageous

____ experienced

____ musher

____ rugged

a. the driver of a dogsled team

b. having a rough, uneven surface

c. a very heavy snowstorm with strong winds

d. a place along a route where vehicles or travelers are counted

e. having skill or knowledge from doing something in the past

f. brave

1. How would a **blizzard** affect driving conditions?

_____

_____

2. What have you done that is **courageous**?

_____

_____

3. Why does a **musher** have to love animals?

_____

_____

4. Why do **experienced** drivers make fewer mistakes?

_____

_____

5. Why is a **checkpoint** a good thing to have in a long race?

_____

_____

Story Map

Main Characters

_____

Setting

_____

Problem Facing Characters (page 37)

_____

_____

Step One (page 39)

_____

_____

Step Two (page 40)

_____

_____

Step Three (page 42)

_____

_____

Solution (pages 49–50)

_____

_____

Name _____

Hero of the Trail

Complete the information for the TV special based on *Akiak*.

TV Sports Special

Title character: _____

Brief description: _____

_____

Second main character: _____

Brief description: _____

_____

Background about the Iditarod: _____

_____

_____

Organization of story: _____

_____

Summary: _____

_____

_____

_____

_____

_____

_____

Universal Knowledge

Read the story. Then complete the chart on the following page.

Saving the Solar System!

Justin stood back, turned on the switch, and watched the planets begin to move. He had worked for months creating a motorized model of the solar system to enter in the science fair. And today was the day. He carried the model out to the car, where his mother was waiting.

Justin tried to get the model into the car without damaging any parts. It didn't fit! "Mom!" Justin almost shouted. "Please! Let's ask Mrs. Kravitz from next door if she'll help with her minivan."

Justin explained his problem to Mrs. Kravitz, who smiled and said, "I'd be honored to help save the universe!"

When they finally reached school, Justin removed the model from the minivan, thanked Mrs. Kravitz, and carried in his project. He took his assigned place and then realized that there was no electrical outlet close enough to plug in his model. And the judging was about to start!

Justin spotted the janitor, Mr. Jackson. Justin asked if he might borrow an extension cord. Mr. Jackson smiled as he handed the cord to Justin and said, "I'm happy to do anything to help the universe."

Justin thanked Mr. Jackson, quickly attached the extension cord, and finally plugged in his model. Just as the judges were stepping up to his area, Justin flipped the switch. The planets slowly began to move, just as they should. Justin sighed with relief. The solar system had been saved.

Name _____

Universal Knowledge

Complete this Problem-Solution Frame for the story "Saving the Solar System."

The Problems That Justin Faces and the Solutions He Finds
Problem 1: _____
_____
Solution 1: _____
_____
_____
Problem 2: _____
_____
Solution 2: _____
_____

If you had been Justin, what would you have done in advance to avoid the problems he faced on the day of the science fair?

_____

_____

What might Justin have done if Mrs. Kravitz and her minivan were unable to transport his project?

_____

_____

Name _____

Adding -er and -est to Adjectives

Add -er to an adjective to compare two people, places, or things:

Willy's team of dogs is fast**er** than the other team.

Add -est to an adjective to compare three or more people, places, or things:

Mick's team is fast**est** of all.

Read each sentence. Change the adjective in parentheses to the correct form as you write it in the puzzle. Remember the spelling rules!

Across

1. People believed Akiak was the (brave) sled dog of all.
3. After the race, Mick was the (happy) musher in Alaska.
4. A dog's undercoat is (fine) than its outer coat.
7. Huskies are not the (friendly) breed of dogs.

Down

2. The ice is (thin) at the edge of the lake than in the middle.
3. The snowfall is (heavy) today than yesterday.
4. Isn't that the (fat) Husky puppy you've ever seen?
5. The cocoa is (hot) than the tea.
6. The sky on the first day was (blue) than a robin's egg.

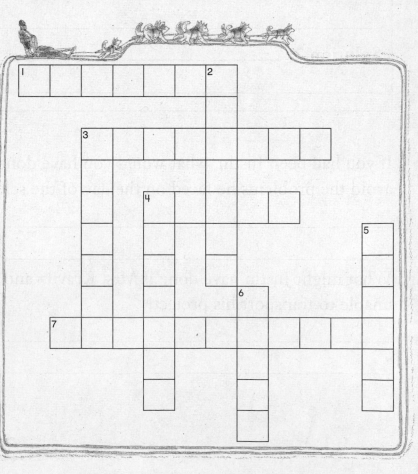

The /ă/, /ā/, /ĕ/, and /ē/ Sounds

Remember that the /ă/ sound is usually spelled *a* followed by a consonant sound. When you hear the /ā/ sound, think of the patterns *a-consonant-e*, *ai*, and *ay*.

/ă/ p**a**st   /ā/ s**a**f**e**, g**ai**n, gr**ay**

Remember that the /ĕ/ sound is usually spelled *e* followed by a consonant sound. When you hear the /ē/ sound, think of the patterns *ea* and *ee*.

/ĕ/ k**e**pt   /ē/ cr**ea**m, sw**ee**t

► In the starred words *break* and *steak*, *ea* spells the /ā/ sound, not the /ē/ sound.

► In the starred words *field* and *chief*, the /ē/ sound is spelled *ie*.

Write each Spelling Word under its vowel sound.

/ă/ Sound	/ĕ/ Sound
_____	_____
_____	_____

/ā/ Sound	/ē/ Sound
_____	_____
_____	_____
_____	_____
_____	_____
_____	_____

Spelling Words

1. gain
2. cream
3. sweet
4. safe
5. past
6. reach
7. kept
8. gray
9. field*
10. break*
11. east
12. shape
13. steep
14. pray
15. pain
16. glass
17. west
18. cheap
19. steak*
20. chief*

Spelling Spree

Name _____

Finding Words Write the Spelling Word hidden in each word below.

1. painting _____
2. reshapes _____
3. cheapest _____
4. screams _____
5. again _____
6. preacher _____
7. sprayer _____
8. pasture _____

1. gain
2. cream
3. sweet
4. safe
5. past
6. reach
7. kept
8. gray
9. field*
10. break*
11. east
12. shape
13. steep
14. pray
15. pain
16. glass
17. west
18. cheap
19. steak*
20. chief*

POSTAGE

Familiar Phrases Write the Spelling Word that completes each phrase.

9. grill a _____
10. found _____ and sound
11. tastes as _____ as honey
12. a big _____ of milk
13. the _____ of police
14. _____ a secret
15. a _____ of wheat

18   Theme 1: **Journeys**

Name _____

Proofreading and Writing

Proofreading Circle the five misspelled Spelling Words in this weather report. Then write each word correctly.

The weather for this week's Iditarod will start off cold and grae. Then a storm front from the wast will bring snow to the area. The snow will be very heavy to the est, up in the mountains. If you're traveling in that area, play it safe! Watch out for ice on the steap hills. We should get a braek in the weather later in the week. The clouds will move away, the sun will return, and the temperature will warm up to just below freezing!

Spelling Words
1. gain
2. cream
3. sweet
4. safe
5. past
6. reach
7. kept
8. gray
9. field*
10. break*
11. east
12. shape
13. steep
14. pray
15. pain
16. glass
17. west
18. cheap
19. steak*
20. chief*

1. _____   4. _____

2. _____   5. _____

3. _____

✏ **Write an Explanation** The Iditarod is a difficult race that requires skill, courage, and lots of training. Do you like snowstorms and sledding? Have you ever trained a dog? Would you like to race in the Iditarod? Why or why not?

On a separate piece of paper, write a paragraph explaining why you would or would not like to take part in the race. Use Spelling Words from the list.

Name _____

Multiple-Meaning Words

> **de•scent** (dǐ sĕnt′) *noun* **1.** Movement from a higher place to a lower one: *the descent of an elevator.* **2.** Downward slope or inclination: *a staircase with a steep descent.* **3.** Ancestry or birth: *That family is of Russian descent.* **4.** A sudden attack: *The bird's descent on the worm was swift.*

For each sentence, choose the correct definition of the underlined word and write its number on the line.

1. The hill's <u>descent</u> was not very steep, so we reached the bottom easily. _____

2. Many people of Inuit <u>descent</u> live in Alaska. _____

3. The explorers had a difficult <u>descent</u> down the rocky mountain. _____

4. The hungry dogs made a quick <u>descent</u> on the food. _____

> **ref•uge** (rĕf′ ūj) *noun* **1.** Shelter or protection from danger: *The frightened cat took refuge under the bed.* **2.** A place providing shelter or protection: *There are many animals in the wildlife refuge.* **3.** A source of comfort or relief: *Listening to music is her refuge when she's feeling sad.*

For each underlined word, choose the correct definition and write its number on the line at the end of the sentence.

5. The injured elephant was sent to a <u>refuge</u> for sick animals. _____

6. During the blizzard, the lost dog found <u>refuge</u> behind a snowdrift. _____

7. After losing the game, the team took <u>refuge</u> in knowing that they played their best. _____

8. The huge tree provided a <u>refuge</u> for the bird's nest. _____

Name _____

Finding Kinds of Sentences

Rewrite each sentence on the lines below, adding the correct end mark. Then write what type of sentence it is.

1. The trail is very long and difficult

    _____

    _____

2. Did Akiak ever win a race before

    _____

    _____

3. How many teams began the race

    _____

    _____

4. What a smart lead dog she is

    _____

    _____

5. Hold on to the dog, please

    _____

    _____

Name _____

Sentences About Alaska

Read the facts below about Alaska, and use the facts to write five sentences. Write at least one command, one question, one statement, and one exclamation.

Facts

- became 49th state in 1959
- largest state of all
- Mt. McKinley: highest mountain in North America
- Yukon River: 2,000 miles long
- many active volcanoes
- midsummer sun shines all night
- capital is Juneau
- Iditarod race in March each year

1. _____

_____

2. _____

_____

3. _____

_____

4. _____

_____

5. _____

_____

Name _____

Capitalizing and Punctuating Sentences

Careful writers capitalize the first word of every sentence and make sure that each sentence has the right end mark. Read the sentences below. Rewrite each sentence, adding capital letters and end marks where needed. Then write what kind of sentence each is.

1. this race was the first one for some dogs

   _____

2. did you ever see the Iditarod race

   _____

3. how fast the sled dogs run

   _____

4. watch the lead dog of the sled team

   _____

5. which team won the race

   _____

Name _____

Planning Chart

Use this chart to help you plan your news article.

Topic of news article: _____

Who?	**What?**
_____	_____
_____	_____
_____	_____
_____	_____
When?	**Where?**
_____	_____
_____	_____
_____	_____
_____	_____
Why?	**How?**
_____	_____
_____	_____
_____	_____
_____	_____

Name _____

Adding Details

From the details given below, choose the detail that you think adds the right information to each sentence and write it in the blank provided.

Through icy water and confusing trails	fifty-eight
a maze of	deep, wet
wait out the storm	From Anchorage to Nome,

1. _____,
   the sled dog teams battled wind, snow, and steep, rugged trails.

2. The race began and one by one, the _____
   teams took off.

3. _____,
   Akiak never got lost, but always found the safest and fastest way.

4. Akiak was limping because the
   _____
   snow had made one of her paws sore.

5. Akiak burrowed into a snowdrift to _____
   _____.

6. Halfway to the checkpoint, Mick's team came upon
   _____ snowmobile tracks.

Name _____

Revising Your Personal Narrative

Reread your story. Put a checkmark in the box for each sentence that describes your paper. Use this page to help you revise.

Rings the Bell

☐ The beginning catches the reader's interest.

☐ All events are focused on a single experience. They are also told in order..

☐ Details and exact words bring the story to life.

☐ My writing sounds like me. It shows how I feel.

☐ Sentences flow smoothly. There are few mistakes.

Getting Stronger

☐ The beginning could be more interesting.

☐ A few events are out of order or unrelated.

☐ More details and exact words are needed.

☐ My voice could be stronger.

☐ Sentences don't flow smoothly. There are some mistakes.

Try Harder

☐ The beginning is missing or weak.

☐ The story is not focused. The order is unclear.

☐ There are no details or exact words.

☐ I can't hear my voice at all.

☐ My sentences are choppy. There are many mistakes.

Name _____

Varying Sentences

**Change these paragraphs in the spaces provided. Each
paragraph should have at least one example of each type of
sentence: declarative, interrogative, command, and exclamatory.**

Balloon Bread
No Sentence Variation

My mom and I made bread. We mixed warm water and flour. We added yeast. We
let the dough rise. The dough kept rising and rising. We baked the bread. It came
out way too light and fluffy — like a balloon. We put in too much yeast. Better luck
next time.

Balloon Bread
Sentence Variation

_____

_____

_____

_____

Junk Food
No Sentence Variation

Am I unusual? Why don't I like junk food? Why do I lose my appetite at fast food
places? Do you like junk food? Does it make you sick? Do you think it's unhealthy?
If so, then why do you eat it? And why does everyone else like it so much?
Why am I so confused?

Junk Food
Sentence Variation

_____

_____

_____

Name _____

Spelling Words

Words Often Misspelled Look for familiar spelling patterns to help you remember how to spell the Spelling Words on this page. Think carefully about the parts that you find hard to spell in each word.

Write the missing letters and apostrophes in the Spelling Words below.

1. ca _____ _____ ot
2. ca _____ _____ _____
3. do _____ _____ _____
4. hav _____ _____ _____ _____
5. w _____ _____ 't
6. w _____ _____ _____ dn't
7. I _____ _____
8. I' _____ _____
9. let _____ _____
10. we _____ _____ _____
11. I _____ _____
12. did _____ _____ _____
13. _____ _____ _____ lock
14. that _____ _____
15. ther _____ _____ _____

Spelling Words

1. cannot
2. can't
3. don't
4. haven't
5. won't
6. wouldn't
7. I'd
8. I'll
9. let's
10. we're
11. I'm
12. didn't
13. o'clock
14. that's
15. there's

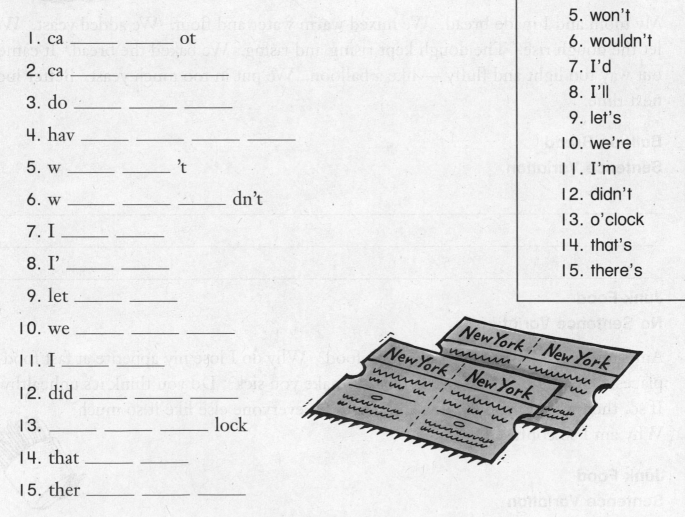

Study List On a separate piece of paper, write each Spelling Word. Check your spelling against the words on the list.

Name _____

Spelling Spree

Write the Spelling Word that fits each clue.

Spelling Words

1. If you're talking about your future, you might use this
   contraction. _____

2-3. This contraction and this word both say you're not able
   to do something. _____

4. A group of people talking about themselves might use
   this contraction. _____

5. This contraction tells you things not to do. _____

6. This contraction can tell time. _____

7. This contraction is the past tense of *doesn't*. _____

8. This contraction is a quick way to say you don't have
   something. _____

9. "I will not" can also be said "I _____."

Spelling Words
1. cannot
2. can't
3. don't
4. haven't
5. won't
6. wouldn't
7. I'd
8. I'll
9. let's
10. we're
11. I'm
12. didn't
13. o'clock
14. that's
15. there's

Find a Rhyme Write a Spelling Word that rhymes with the
underlined word. Be sure it makes sense.

10. _____ trying to find words that <u>rhyme</u>.

11. Ina <u>couldn't</u> pay attention to the movie because Ben
   _____ leave her alone.

12. If my ankle wasn't hurting me, _____ try to <u>ride</u>
   that horse.

13. My sister said _____ a kid in her class who eats
   four <u>pears</u> for lunch every day.

14. Well, _____ see who <u>gets</u> to the end of the block the quickest.

15. I think _____ the girl who <u>bats</u> from both sides of the plate.

*did not =
didn't
I will =
I'll
of the clock =
o'clock*

Theme 1: **Journeys**   29

Proofreading and Writing

Proofreading Circle the five misspelled Spelling Words in this advertisement. Then write each word correctly.

Think you dont have enough money to take a journey? Think again! With Express Airlines' new sale fares, you ca'nt afford not to travel! We've got flights going all over the country, at prices you won't believe. You can leave any time between six oclock in the morning and midnight. And we'ere proud to offer the best service of any airline out there. So you see, theres no reason not to fly with us!

Spelling Words

1. cannot
2. can't
3. don't
4. haven't
5. won't
6. wouldn't
7. I'd
8. I'll
9. let's
10. we're
11. I'm
12. didn't
13. o'clock
14. that's
15. there's

1. _____
2. _____
3. _____
4. _____
5. _____

➤ **Journey Sentences** Suppose you were going on a journey to a place where they spoke a foreign language. What are some things you might want to know how to say once you got there?

On a separate piece of paper, write five sentences you would want to know for your journey. Use Spelling Words from the list.

Name _____

Traveling Words

Write the words next to their definitions. Unscramble the circled letters to answer the question that follows.

Vocabulary

bewildered	homeland	longed
marveled	reminded	surrounded

1. country you were born in

2. wanted very much

3. became filled with wonder

4. puzzled greatly

5. made someone remember

6. put all around

What is a word for someone who takes a trip?

☐ ☐ c ☐ t ☐ ☐ ☐ ☐ ☐

Name _____

Word Web

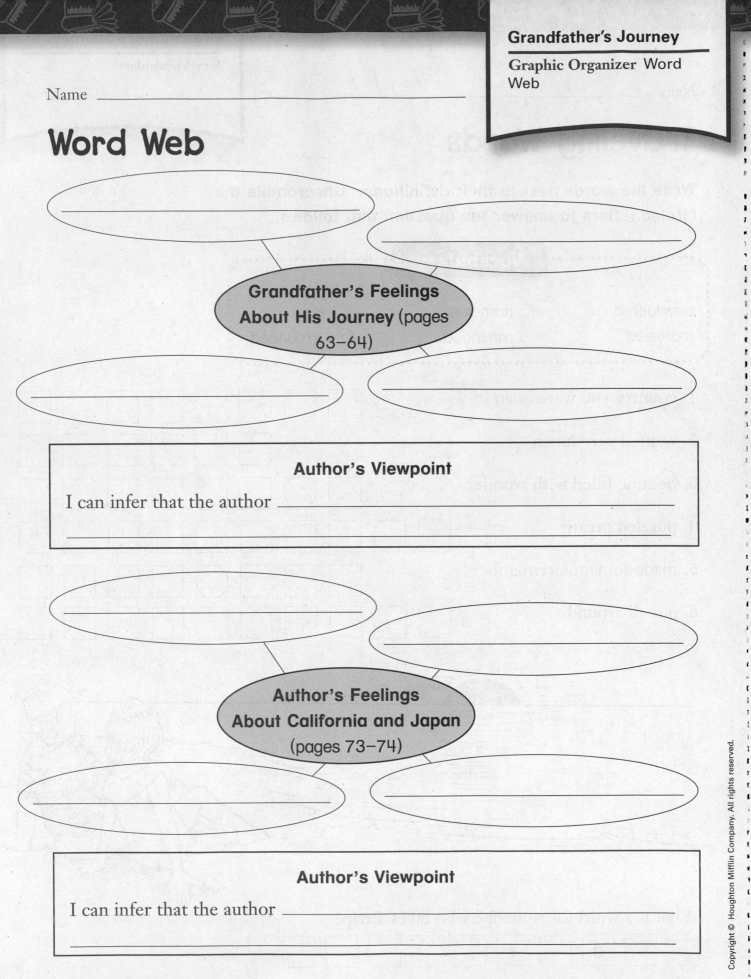

Grandfather's Feelings
About His Journey (pages
63–64)

Author's Viewpoint

I can infer that the author _____

_____

Author's Feelings
About California and Japan
(pages 73–74)

Author's Viewpoint

I can infer that the author _____

_____

Name _____

Grandfather's Diary

Help grandfather write his diary by filling in the blanks.

Entry 1—The Pacific Ocean is huge. Once we left Japan, we did

not see land again _____

Entry 2—America is as big as the ocean, and there is much to see.

I am excited and delighted by _____

_____

_____

Entry 3—My favorite place is California because it has _____

_____

Entry 4—I returned to Japan to _____ and then

settled in _____

Entry 5—I miss my _____ and

homeland, so when my daughter is nearly grown, I take my family

_____

Name _____

A Moving View

Read the story. Then answer the questions on the following page.

Saying Good-bye, Saying Hello

"Hurry up, Anna! We've got a long drive ahead of us! We've got to get started now!" Recently, all my father seemed to do was shout. All I did was mope and complain. It only seemed fair because we were moving away from our home and from the friends I loved. As our car pulled away from the curb, I waved weakly at Andrea and Kelly. They were my very best friends in the whole world. And even though they promised to write every day, I knew our friendship might never be the same.

On the long drive from Indiana to New Mexico, my father talked and talked and talked about how happy we were going to be in our new home near my grandparents. But I didn't care. All I could think of was losing my whole life.

When I opened my eyes, the gentle desert sunlight smiled hello to me. We turned down a dirt road and out of a sand-colored house came running my grandparents and many other smiling relatives. My cousin Sunita pulled me away from the crowd and told me that we would be going to the same school and might even be in the same class. She also told me her favorite jokes, and I started laughing really hard.

I thought to myself, "Maybe I only left a part of my life behind. Maybe this next part will also be wonderful."

Name _____

A Moving View continued

Answer these questions that refer to the story "Saying Good-bye, Saying Hello."

What phrases does the narrator use to describe moving from Indiana?

_____

What can you infer about the narrator's feelings toward Indiana?

_____

_____

What phrases describe the narrator's experience in New Mexico?

_____

How does the narrator feel about New Mexico?

_____

_____

What is the author's purpose in writing this story?

_____

_____

 Theme 1: **Journeys**   35

Name _____

Suffixes *-ly* and *-y*

Add -*ly* or -*y* to a base word to mean "in the manner of."

high/high**ly**   rain/rain**y**

When a base word ends in a consonant and *y*, change the *y* to *i*
before adding -*ly*.

speed**y**/speed**ily**   eas**y**/eas**ily**

When a base word ends in a short vowel and a consonant, double
the consonant before adding -*y*.

fog/fog**gy**   tin/tin**ny**

**Choose one of the pictures to write about in a short paragraph.
Add -*y* or -*ly* to at least four of the words under the picture. Use
them in your paragraph.**

| chill | happy | quick | salt | | sad | merry | luck | sun |
| final | fog | sudden | weary | | silk | lone | hungry | soft |

_____

_____

_____

_____

36   Theme 1: **Journeys**

Name _____

The /ĭ/, /ī/, /ŏ/, and /ō/ Sounds

Remember that the /ĭ/ sound is often spelled *i* followed by a consonant sound. When you hear the /ī/ sound, think of the patterns *i*-consonant-*e*, *igh*, and *i*.

> /ĭ/ **st**i**ll**   /ī/ cr**ime**, fl**igh**t, gr**i**nd

► In the starred words *build* and *built*, the /ĭ/ sound is spelled *ui*.

Remember that the /ŏ/ sound is usually spelled *o* followed by a consonant sound. When you hear the /ō/ sound, think of the patterns *o*-consonant-*e*, *oa*, *ow*, and *o*.

> /ŏ/ **o**dd   /ō/ wr**ote**, c**oa**st, sn**ow**, g**o**ld

Write each Spelling Word under its vowel sound.

Spelling Words

1. snow
2. grind
3. still
4. coast
5. odd
6. crime
7. gold
8. wrote
9. flight
10. build*
11. broke
12. blind
13. folk
14. grown
15. shock
16. ripe
17. coal
18. inch
19. sigh
20. built*

/ĭ/ Sound

_____
_____
_____

/ī/ Sound

_____
_____
_____
_____
_____
_____

/ŏ/ Sound

_____

/ō/ Sound

_____
_____
_____
_____
_____
_____

Name _____

Spelling Spree

Letter Math Write a Spelling Word by adding and subtracting letters from the words below.

Example: sm + poke – p = *smoke*

1. s + high – h = _____

2. b + quilt – q = _____

3. c + goal – g = _____

4. gr + blown – bl = _____

5. r + swipe – sw = _____

6. f + yolk – y = _____

7. cr + slime – sl = _____

Inside Switch Change one letter on the inside of each word to make a Spelling Word. Write the words.

Example: drip *drop*

8. grand   _____

9. shack   _____

10. blond   _____

11. itch   _____

12. old   _____

13. brake   _____

14. stall   _____

15. write   _____

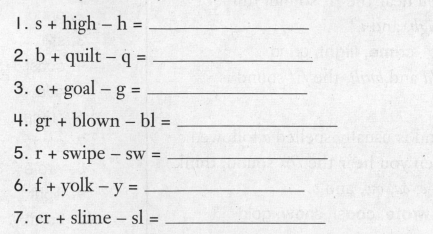

Spelling Words
1. snow
2. grind
3. still
4. coast
5. odd
6. crime
7. gold
8. wrote
9. flight
10. build*
11. broke
12. blind
13. folk
14. grown
15. shock
16. ripe
17. coal
18. inch
19. sigh
20. built*

Name _____

Proofreading and Writing

Proofreading Circle the five misspelled Spelling Words in the tour schedule. Then write each word correctly.

California Dream Tour!

Day 1: Your plane lands in Los Angeles. Tour this famous city. Then ride along the area's beautiful cost.

Day 2: Spend a relaxing day on the beach at Santa Monica. Sun, surf, or bild your own sandcastle.

Day 3: Ride by bus to Yosemite National Park. Play in the sno on the mountains, then rest up at the lodge.

Day 4: Visit Sacramento. Explore the spot where golde was discovered in 1848. Pan for any of the precious metal that might still be left in the mountain streams.

Day 5: Take a bus to beautiful San Francisco and catch your flite home.

1. _____   4. _____

2. _____   5. _____

3. _____

Spelling Words

1. snow
2. grind
3. still
4. coast
5. odd
6. crime
7. gold
8. wrote
9. flight
10. build*
11. broke
12. blind
13. folk
14. grown
15. shock
16. ripe
17. coal
18. inch
19. sigh
20. built*

Write a Contest Entry A local travel agency is having a contest. First prize is a trip to anywhere in the United States. Where would you go if you had the opportunity? Would it be San Francisco? The Rocky Mountains? The Florida Everglades?

On a separate piece of paper, write a paragraph telling where you would go if you won the contest and why you want to go there. Use Spelling Words from the list.

Theme 1: **Journeys**   39

Name _____

What's the Order?

Put each group of words in alphabetical order. Write the words
on the lines provided.

week   _____

war   _____

where   _____

warbler   _____

when   _____

towering   _____

travel   _____

thought   _____

there   _____

trip   _____

steamship   _____

seacoast   _____

strong   _____

songbird   _____

sunlight   _____

Name _____

Identifying Subjects and Predicates

Copy each sentence and draw a vertical line between the complete subject and the complete predicate of each sentence. Then circle the simple subject and underline the simple predicate.

1. Grandfather met many different people in his travels.

   _____

2. The seacoast of California appealed to him.

   _____

3. The young man found a bride in Japan.

   _____

4. The two people made their home in San Francisco.

   _____

5. Memories of Japan filled Grandfather's mind.

   _____

Name _____

Connecting Subjects and Predicates

Draw a line connecting each subject in Column 1 with the predicate in Column 2 that makes the most sense. Put the two sentence parts together and write the whole sentence on the lines below. Then circle the simple subject and underline the simple predicate of each sentence you wrote.

Column 1	**Column 2**
1. The old man	a. went back home with him.
2. Songbirds	b. laughed with him.
3. The man's family	c. reminded him of Japan.
4. His old friends	d. married a man in Japan.
5. The couple's daughter	e. remembered his homeland fondly.

1. _____

2. _____

3. _____

4. _____

5. _____

Name _____

Sentence Combining

Use the joining word in parentheses to combine each pair of sentences below with a compound subject or a compound predicate. Write the new sentence. Then circle the compound part in your new sentence and write whether it is a compound subject or a compound predicate.

1. The grandfather talked with his grandson.

   The grandfather told stories about California. (and)

   _____

   _____

2. Grandfather raised songbirds.

   Grandfather loved their songs. (and)

   _____

   _____

3. Warblers were his favorite birds.

   Silvereyes were his favorite birds. (and)

   _____

   _____

4. Bombs fell.

   Bombs ruined many homes. (and)

   _____

   _____

5. The old man lost a home.

   His family lost a home. (and)

   _____

   _____

Name _____

What Are My Thoughts?

Title of Story _____

Response Journal

Use the questions below to write your responses to the story.

How do I feel about the events of the story?

_____

_____

How do I feel about the main character?

_____

_____

What do I like best about the story? What do I like least?

_____

_____

What do I think will happen next in the story?

_____

_____

What puzzles me about the story?

_____

_____

Which character in the story is most like me? Why?

_____

_____

What else would I like to say about the story?

_____

_____

Name _____

Giving Examples

Improve each of the following response journal entries by adding examples based on *Grandfather's Journey*. Write your examples on the lines provided.

1. If I were to travel in a foreign country, I would like to do and see many things.

   _____

   _____

2. If I lived in a foreign country, I would miss many things about the United States.

   _____

   _____

   _____

3. When I was the age of the small boy in the story, I too had a favorite thing to do on a weekend with my family.

   _____

   _____

   _____

4. Some things puzzle me about the people in the story.

   _____

   _____

   _____

5. I have some class project ideas related to Japan.

   _____

   _____

Name _____

Seaworthy Words

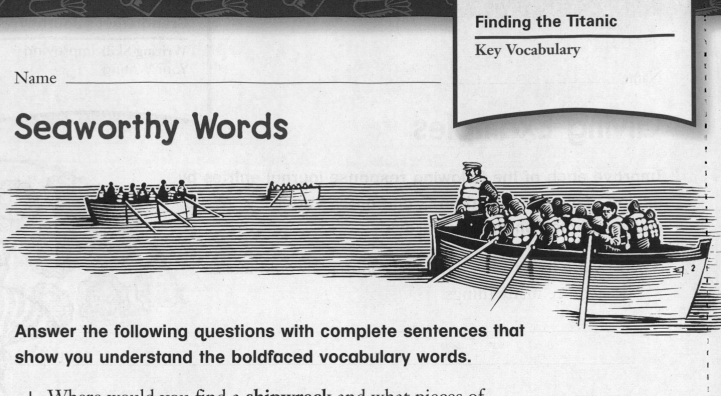

Answer the following questions with complete sentences that show you understand the boldfaced vocabulary words.

1. Where would you find a **shipwreck** and what pieces of **wreckage** might you find there?

   _____

   _____

2. Can an **unsinkable** ship be made? Why or why not?

   _____

   _____

3. Where would you like to take a **voyage**? What would you do on the trip?

   _____

   _____

4. Where might you find **plaques**? Why would they be there?

   _____

   _____

5. What would rescued **survivors** look like?

   _____

   _____

Name _____

Organizational Outline

I. Chapter One

A. Main Idea: _____

B. What the pictures show: _____

_____

II. Chapter Two

A. Main Idea: _____

_____

B. What the pictures show: _____

_____

III. Chapter Three

A. Main Idea: _____

_____

B. What the pictures show: _____

_____

IV. Chapter Four

A. Main Idea: _____

_____

B. What the pictures show: _____

_____

V. Chapter Six

A. Main Idea: _____

_____

B. What the pictures show: _____

_____

Name _____

Time Goes On

Complete the sentences about the time line. Then answer the question below.

1910

April 10, 1912 The *Titanic*, a brand new luxury liner as tall as an _____, set sail from Southampton, England.

April 15, 1912 The *Titanic* crashed into an _____. Many people were still on board when the giant ship _____.

1950

August 25, 1985 The *Titanic* lay _____ on the ocean floor, too deep for any diver, but the *Argo*, an _____ equipped with a video camera, searched and found the *Titanic*.

August 31, 1985 The first piece of the *Titanic* found by the cameras was a _____ used to drive the ship's engines.

1980

1985

July 13, 1986 The robot, _____, photographed the shiny chandelier that hung over the Grand Staircase.

1990

How is it possible that the *Titanic* could not be found for seventy-five years but can now be seen and photographed?

_____

_____

Name _____

Organizing the Wreckage

Read the article. Then answer the questions on the following page.

Why Did the *Lusitania* Sink?

1. **Exploring the Wreck**

    Dr. Robert Ballard, the explorer who discovered the *Titanic*, decided to look for the *Lusitania*. He wanted to find out what caused the huge explosion onboard the ship. He also wanted to know why it sank so quickly. Using high-technology submarines and robots, his crew explored the wreck. What they found was a huge hole in the ship's bow. The hole was right where there were compartments used to store coal, which fueled the ship. And to their amazement, the hole looked like it was blasted from the inside out!

2. **Setting Sail**

    On May 7, 1915, the British ocean liner *Lusitania* was sailing off the coast of Ireland. It was on its way from New York to England. In Europe, World War I was being fought, but no one thought that a submarine would sink an ocean liner filled with passengers. On that day, however, a submarine launched a torpedo toward the *Lusitania*. When the torpedo struck the ship, there was a huge explosion. The ship sank in less than 20 minutes, and many passengers and crew lost their lives.

Time Line: The Wreck of the *Lusitania*

0 min.	2 min.	2 min., 3 sec.		17 min.
torpedo fired	torpedo strikes ship	coal dust explodes a hole in ship	seawater pours into ship	*Lusitania* sinks

Name _____

Organizing the Wreckage

continued

Answer the following questions about the sinking of the *Lusitania*.

1. What are this article's special features?

    _____

2. What is the purpose of the visual aid?

    _____

    _____

3. How well does this visual aid work? Explain your answer.

    _____

    _____

4. What would you do to better organize this article? Explain
    your answer.

    _____

    _____

    _____

    _____

    _____

Name _____

Syllabication

All words contain **syllables**, which are smaller parts you hear when you say a word out loud. For example, the name *Titanic* contains three syllables: /tī - TAN - ĭ|k|/. Some long words such as *thought* have only one syllable.

| dreamed | largest | passenger |
| dreamed (one) | larg-est (two) | pas-sen-ger (three) |

Use what you've learned about syllabication to break each word into syllables. Rewrite the word to show the syllables. (The first one is done for you.) Then arrange the words with three syllables to make an exciting newspaper headline from 1985.

OCEAN DAILY TIMES

_____ _____

_____ _____ !

1. cabin **cab-in**

2. explore _____

3. signals _____

4. underneath _____

5. huge _____

6. bigger _____

7. Atlantic _____

8. iceberg _____

9. discovered _____

10. sinking _____

11. straight _____

12. Titanic _____

Name _____

The /ŭ/, /yoō/, and /oō/ Sounds

Remember that the /ŭ/ sound is usually spelled *u* followed by a consonant sound. When you hear the /yoō/ or the /oō/ sound, think of the patterns *u*-consonant-*e*, *ew*, *ue*, and *ui*.

/ŭ/ br**u**sh   /yoō/ and /oō/ t**u**be, f**ew**, tr**ue**, j**ui**ce

► In the starred word *done*, the /ŭ/ sound is spelled *o*. In the starred word *truth*, the /oō/ sound is spelled *u*.

Write each Spelling Word under its vowel sound.

Spelling Words

1. brush
2. juice
3. fruit
4. tube
5. lunch
6. crumb
7. few
8. true
9. truth*
10. done*
11. suit
12. pump
13. due
14. dull
15. tune
16. blew
17. trunk
18. sum
19. glue
20. threw

/ŭ/ Sound

_____

_____

_____

_____

_____

_____

_____

_____

/yoō/ or /oō/ Sound

_____

_____

_____

_____

_____

_____

_____

_____

_____

_____

_____

_____

Name _____

Proofreading and Writing

Proofreading Circle the five misspelled Spelling Words in this interview. Then write each word correctly on the lines below.

Reporter: I'm writing a story about the
   Titanic. Can you answer a fue questions?

Scientist: I'll try. Do you mind if I eat lunch while
   we talk?

Reporter: No, I don't mind at all. Tell me, is it troo
   that the ship broke in two before it sank?

Scientist: Yes, that is correct. After the impact the crew
   tried to pomp the water out, but it was no use. The
   iceberg had dun too much damage.

Reporter: Can you som up for us what you've learned
   from the *Titanic*?

Scientist: There's no such thing as an unsinkable ship.

1. _____   4. _____

2. _____   5. _____

3. _____

✏️➤ **Write a Story** Have you ever wondered what you would do in an unfamiliar or dangerous situation? Write the beginning of an adventure story. The setting could be anywhere—an underwater cave or a galaxy far, far away.

On a separate sheet of paper, write the opening paragraph for your story. Use Spelling Words from the list.

Name _____

Spelling Spree

Word Search Write the Spelling Word that is hidden in each sentence.

Example: We found shelter in a small gras<u>s hut</u>. *shut*

1. Don't trip over the cable wire.
2. The two sisters sang a duet.
3. Beth reworded her opening paragraph.
4. You can fill that tub easily with a garden hose.
5. The snowstorm was not unexpected.
6. The frisky lamb rushed to the pasture.
7. The explorers found a small uncharted island.
8. That ruthless villain must be punished!

1. _____   5. _____
2. _____   6. _____
3. _____   7. _____
4. _____   8. _____

Alphabet Puzzler Write the Spelling Word that would appear alphabetically between each pair of words below.

9. forest, _____, gate
10. castle, _____, cute
11. trumpet, _____, trust
12. garden, _____, hard
13. duke, _____, dusty
14. jam, _____, justice
15. robot, _____, suitcase

Spelling Words

1. brush
2. juice
3. fruit
4. tube
5. lunch
6. crumb
7. few
8. true
9. truth*
10. done*
11. suit
12. pump
13. due
14. dull
15. tune
16. blew
17. trunk
18. sum
19. glue
20. threw

Theme 1: **Journeys**   53

Name _____

Find a Better Word

**In each sentence, replace the underlined
word with a better word or words. Choose
your word or words from the thesaurus
entries below and write them on the line.
Remember that more than one word may
be correct in some cases.**

1. **bottom:** base, floor, depths, foot, ground
   Many ships have sunk to the <u>bottom</u> of the ocean as a result
   of accidents or storms at sea.

   _____

2. **group:** band, body, crew, crowd, gang, heap
   There was a large <u>group</u> of people on the dock waving good-bye
   to the passengers.

   _____

3. **recovery:** bailout, release, rescue, salvage
   In the distance the survivors could see the <u>recovery</u> ship.

   _____

4. **hard:** stable, solid, sound, stout, sturdy, tough
   The <u>hard</u> deck of the ship felt good beneath her feet.

   _____

5. **dangerous:** adventurous, bad, perilous, risky, serious
   Alvin's first trip to video the wreckage was <u>dangerous</u>.

   _____

Name _____

Connecting Compound Sentences

Underline the two sentences that have been combined in the compound sentences below. Then circle the conjunction that joins them.

1. The *Titanic* had nine decks, and it was as tall as an eleven-story building.

2. The Becker family boarded the ship, and a steward helped them to find their room.

3. Ruth took the elevator to the lowest level, and she found a swimming pool there.

4. Ruth wanted to go on deck, but the weather was too cold.

5. The ship was traveling fast, but ice could slow it down.

Name _____

Compound Sentences in a Letter

Read this student's letter to a friend. On the lines below, write compound sentences.

Dear Sylvia,

   I just read about the sinking of the *Titanic*. The author of the piece is a scientist. His name is Robert Ballard, and he explores the oceans. Ballard has found undersea mountains, but he is also interested in sunken ships. He searched the Atlantic Ocean for the *Titanic*, and his crew finally found it. The ship was on its first trip to the United States in 1912. It was supposed to be unsinkable, but it hit an iceberg. The iceberg tore a hole in the hull of the ship, and the ship sank.

              Your friend,

              Janice

_____

_____

_____

_____

_____

_____

_____

_____

Name _____

Writing Compound Sentences

Good writers often combine two sentences with related ideas into a compound sentence. Read the following pairs of sentences. Then rewrite each pair by combining the sentences into a single compound sentence, adding one of the joining words *and* or *but*. Punctuate the sentences correctly.

1. The three-man crew climbed into the tiny submarine.
   It slowly went down to the ocean floor.

   _____

   _____

2. The captain looked out the window. A black wall of steel
   appeared.

   _____

   _____

3. He looked for the yellow letters "Titanic." They were covered
   over with rust.

   _____

   _____

4. The little robot was steered into a hole in the deck. Soon its
   camera was taking pictures of the wreck.

   _____

   _____

Name _____

Writing an Answer to a Question

For each question, write the answer on the lines provided. Write the
start of the answer on the first answer line. Write the rest of the
answer on the other answer lines. The first one is done for you.

Question: Would you enjoy a camping trip?

Start of answer: Turn question into statement

I would enjoy a camping trip because

**Rest of answer: Facts that complete the statement and answer
the question asked.**

I enjoy outdoor activities such as hiking, rafting, and walking in the forest.

Question: Would you enjoy a train trip?

Start of answer: Turn question into statement

_____ because

**Rest of answer: Facts that complete the statement and answer
the question asked.**

_____

_____

_____

Question: Would you enjoy a trip on an ocean liner?

Start of answer: Turn question into statement

_____ because

**Rest of answer: Facts that complete the statement and answer
the question asked.**

_____

_____

_____

Name _____

Writing Complete Sentences

Incomplete sentences can sink your writing, so make sure you know them when you see them! Mark each of these items as follows: If it is an incomplete sentence because it is missing a subject or a predicate, write an *X* in the "Sink" column. If it is complete write an *X* in the "Swim" column.

	Sink	**Swim**
Example: The *Titanic*, the largest ship afloat.	X	
1. Sailed from Southampton, England, to New York.		
2. Ruth Becker was excited about traveling on the beautiful ship.		
3. Ruth peeked inside an open door to a first-class cabin.		
4. The Beckers and other passengers in the lounge.		
5. Forgot their life belts.		
6. The *Titanic*'s twenty lifeboats.		
7. She asked to get into the lifeboat.		
8. Ruth Becker stood in the lifeboat.		
9. Many survivors' hands.		
10. Was unwilling to speak about the disaster.		

Name _____

Railroad Words

Write an original story using the vocabulary words.
The words may be used in any order. Be sure to
give your story a title.

Vocabulary

conductor
depot
jolting
lurching
platform
satchels

Name _____

Detail Map

	Details
Waiting for the train	
Riding the train	

Name _____

The Train Ride

**Look at the summary of the Ingalls family's train ride.
Draw a line through each mistake you find and correct it
on the line to the right.**

Laura and her family are traveling by train to meet their

grandmother in a place far from Plum Creek called Golden

Lake. The family has quite a distance to go, so they have to

take a train. Travel by train is slower than traveling by

horse and buggy, so everyone knows it will be a safe ride.

Ma gets the family to the station 10 minutes early. The

train arrives at the station, and everyone climbs on board.

Because of Mary's blindness, Laura describes the car and

passengers for her. The brakeman comes by and punches

little holes in everyone's ticket. Laura watches a man go

down the aisle to get water. He turns a handle and water

flows into a paper cup. Laura goes to get some water

without Ma's permission and has a hard time walking in the

moving train. Laura brings back drinks of water for

Carrie and Mary. After a while a boy appears in the

aisle selling popcorn from a basket. Ma buys some as a

special treat on their first train ride. Suddenly it's noon

and the train ride is over.

Name _____

A Hospital Chart

Read the story. Then complete the Detail Chart on the following page.

"Please, Mom, Tell Me We're Not There Yet!"

When I was little and we were on a car trip, I would ask, "Mom, are we there, yet?" every five minutes. But just last week we went on a car trip and I kept saying, "Please, Mom, tell me we're not there yet!" Why? Mom was driving me to the hospital's emergency room!

It all started on the soccer field. After two minutes of play I fell, grabbing at my stomach. Coach Toth immediately stopped the game. Somehow I made it over to the bench on the sidelines where my mother anxiously waited. My mother and Coach Toth carried me to the car.

I remember looking out the car window on the way to the hospital trying to keep my mind off the pain in my stomach. I saw that someone had painted a house we used to live in a sickening shade of green. I saw the tree that I once fell out of and broke my arm. Then I started to sweat like crazy.

At the emergency room, they kept us waiting only a short time, but it seemed like forever as the pain grew worse. Suddenly a doctor appeared. He seemed to be about eight feet tall. He asked me some questions and felt the sore place on my stomach. I yelled. He asked my mom if I still had my appendix. She told him yes. He said, "Well, she won't for long," and smiled at me. A nurse gave me a shot. The next thing I knew I was wide awake in a hospital room—minus one appendix!

A Hospital Chart continued

Complete these Detail Charts for the story "Please, Mom, Tell
Me We're Not There Yet!"

Before the Hospital	**More Important Details**
	_____
	_____
	_____
	_____
	Less Important Details
	_____
	_____
	_____
At the Hospital	**More Important Details**
	_____
	_____
	_____
	_____
	Less Important Details
	_____
	_____
	_____

Name _____

Word Roots *tele* and *rupt*

Tele and *rupt* are word roots. They have meaning but cannot stand alone. *Tele* means "distance" or "over a distance." *Rupt* means "break."

telescope   television   interrupt   abrupt

Complete each sentence with a word from the box. Use a dictionary to check word meanings if you are not sure which word to choose.

televise	telescope	telegraph	telephone
interrupt	abrupt	disruptive	bankrupt

1. Please don't _____ the conductor when he's taking tickets.

2. One of the astronomers carried her _____ on the train.

3. Is the noise from the dining car _____?

4. Many railroads went _____ when the automobile became popular.

5. Will they _____ the first run of the new high-speed train?

6. Call me on the _____ when you reach the station.

7. The train came to an _____ stop when someone pulled the emergency brake.

8. Before the invention of the _____, Pony Express was one way to send messages quickly.

Name _____

Homophones

Homophones are words that sound alike but have different meanings and spellings. When you write a homophone, be sure to spell the word that has the meaning you want.

/stēl/   st**ee**l   a metal made from iron and carbon

/stēl/   st**ea**l   to take without having permission

Write each Spelling Word under the matching sound.

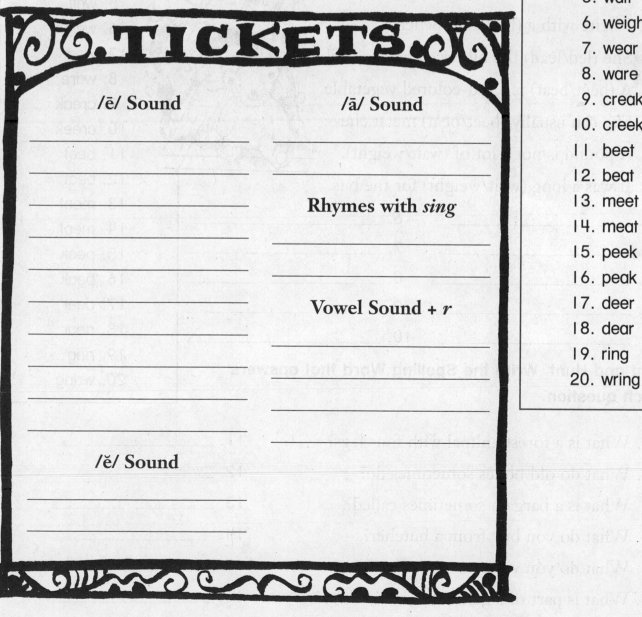

TICKETS

/ē/ Sound

_____
_____
_____
_____
_____
_____
_____
_____
_____

/ĕ/ Sound

_____

/ā/ Sound

_____
_____

Rhymes with *sing*

_____
_____

Vowel Sound + *r*

_____
_____

1. steel
2. steal
3. lead
4. led
5. wait
6. weight
7. wear
8. ware
9. creak
10. creek
11. beet
12. beat
13. meet
14. meat
15. peek
16. peak
17. deer
18. dear
19. ring
20. wring

Name _____

Spelling Spree

Double Trouble Circle the correct Spelling Word.
Write the words on the lines.

1. Please (ring/wring) the clothes dry.

2. I heard the bell (ring/wring).

3. In winter I (wear/ware) a scarf.

4. Those cabinets hold cooking (wear/ware).

5. I write with a (led/lead) pencil.

6. She (led/lead) the hikers along the trail.

7. A (beet/beat) is a red-colored vegetable.

8. She can usually (beet/beat) me at chess.

9. A pound is not a lot of (wait/weight).

10. It was a long (wait/weight) for the bus.

Spelling Words

1. steel
2. steal
3. lead
4. led
5. wait
6. weight
7. wear
8. ware
9. creak
10. creek
11. beet
12. beat
13. meet
14. meat
15. peek
16. peak
17. deer
18. dear
19. ring
20. wring

1. _____   6. _____

2. _____   7. _____

3. _____   8. _____

4. _____   9. _____

5. _____   10. _____

Hint and Hunt Write the Spelling Word that answers
each question.

11. What is a forest animal with four legs?   11. _____

12. What do old bones sometimes do?   12. _____

13. What is a bargain sometimes called?   13. _____

14. What do you buy from a butcher?   14. _____

15. What do you write to start a letter?   15. _____

16. What is part of a game that babies love?   16. _____

Name _____

Proofreading and Writing

Proofreading Circle the four misspelled Spelling Words in this poster. Then write each word correctly.

See the West the Easy Way!

All aboard! Come to the untamed West, where deer, elk, and buffalo still roam the range. Travel on to San Francisco, where the mountains meat the sea. Ride the stel rails from St. Louis all the way to the Pacific Ocean. Cross every valley, river, and creak with ease. See every canyon and snowy peek from the comfort of your passenger seat. Don't wait another minute — get your train tickets today!

Spelling Words

1. steel
2. steal
3. lead
4. led
5. wait
6. weight
7. wear
8. ware
9. creak
10. creek
11. beet
12. beat
13. meet
14. meat
15. peek
16. peak
17. deer
18. dear
19. ring
20. wring

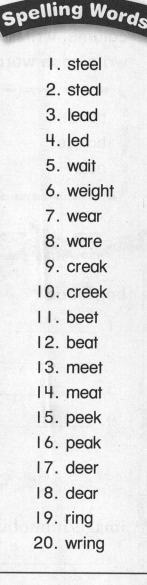

1. _____   3. _____

2. _____   4. _____

Write a List of Rules Laura and her sisters were very careful to behave properly on the train. Have you ever been on a bus, a train, or in any public place where people have behaved in a rude or improper way? How did it make you feel? Think of some rules to remember when sharing a public place with other people.

On a separate sheet of paper, write five rules of good behavior to follow in public places. Use Spelling Words from the list.

Name _____

Find the Guide Words

**Match each word with the correct guide words. In the first
column, write each word under the correct guide words. Then
write each word in alphabetical order between the guide words.**

bond	boil	immediate
boggle	immense	imagine
bold	imitate	

bog/bone   **bog**

1. _____   _____

2. _____   _____

3. _____   _____

4. _____   _____

                                                bone

image/immobile   **image**

1. _____   _____

2. _____   _____

3. _____   _____

4. _____   _____

                                                immobile

Name _____

Finding Common Nouns

Read each sentence, and look for common nouns. Then write each common noun on the lines provided.

1. People waited on the platform for the train.

   _____

2. A traveler rode along at a speed of twenty miles an hour.

   _____

3. The conductor punched holes in the tickets.

   _____

4. Many weeks and months had gone by.

   _____

5. The family sat on a bench in the station.

   _____

6. The woman bought the tickets with money from her pocketbook.

   _____

7. Her dress had a collar and a cuff on each sleeve.

   _____

8. One daughter had long hair with braids and a bow.

   _____

9. Black smoke and white steam came out of the smokestack.

   _____

10. The passengers gathered up their bags and packages.

   _____

Name _____

Choosing Common Nouns

In each sentence, fill in the blank with a noun from the
box. Then, on the following line, write whether the
noun you chose names a person, a place, or a thing.

| weeks | holes | conductor | windows |

1. The _____ smiled.

   _____

2. The _____ on the train were clear.

   _____

3. He punched _____ in the tickets.

   _____

4. Many _____ had gone by before the trip.

   _____

Write two examples of each type of common noun.

Person	Place	Thing
5. _____	7. _____	9. _____
6. _____	8. _____	10. _____

**Use one of the common nouns you wrote for each category to
write your own sentence.**

_____

_____

Name _____

Writing Nouns in a Series

Using Commas in a Series Good writers often combine ideas. Sometimes a sentence will have three or more words of the same kind that follow one another in a series. When three or more words are written in a series, a joining word comes before the last word, and the words are separated by commas.

Read each group of sentences. Then combine the sentences into one sentence with words in a series. Add commas where they are needed. Write your sentences on the lines below.

1. a. People carried satchels.
   b. People carried handbags.
   c. People carried packages.

   _____

   _____

2. a. Out the train window, Laura could see houses.
   b. Out the train window, Laura could see barns.
   c. Out the train window, Laura could see haystacks.

   _____

   _____

3. a. The candy was red.
   b. The candy was yellow.
   c. The candy was striped.

   _____

   _____

4. a. Ma gave the boy a nickel.
   b. Ma gave the boy three pennies.
   c. Ma gave the boy two dimes.

   _____

   _____

Writing a Friendly Letter

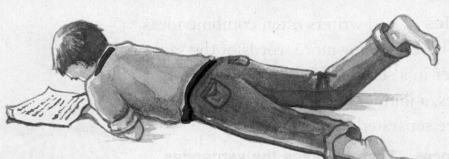

The Person I Am Writing To:

My Address:

The Date:

My Greeting:

My Purpose in Writing:

The Most Important Thing I Want to Say:

Important Details I Want to Include:

My Closing:

Name _____

Using Commas in Dates and Places

In the following letter, add commas as necessary in dates and place names.

Paducah Kentucky

September 14 1878

Dear Cousin Ethan,

    I am so happy to hear that you are doing well at your new homestead. The town of Tracy South Dakota is very lucky to have someone as hardworking as you!

    In your letter of April 23 1878 you described a family on the train you took to Tracy. There were several daughters. Did you ever meet them?

    Now that you are settled I would like to come visit you. I can take a train from Cincinnati Ohio all the way to Tracy If I arrive on May 4 1879 will you meet me at the station?

Your cousin,

Elizabeth

Name _____

Words on a Bird Tour

Write the words next to their definitions. Unscramble the circled letters to answer the question that follows.

Vocabulary

sensation
turbulent
precious
perch
hindrance
fluttered

1. flapped quickly

☐ ☐ ☐ ☐ ☐ ☐ Ⓞ ☐ ☐

2. a feeling

☐ ☐ ☐ ☐ Ⓞ ☐ ☐ ☐ ☐

3. shaken roughly

☐ ☐ ☐ Ⓞ ☐ ☐ ☐ ☐ ☐

4. a place for a bird to sit

☐ ☐ Ⓞ ☐ ☐

5. very valuable

☐ ☐ ☐ ☐ ☐ Ⓞ ☐ ☐

6. an obstacle

Ⓞ ☐ ☐ ☐ ☐ ☐ ☐ ☐ ☐

Where do ships go when they come to New York City?

☐ ☐ ☐ ☐ ☐ ☐

Name _____

Two Trips

	Chester Cricket's Pigeon Ride	The Parcel Post Kid
Main character		
Setting		
Character that leads the main character on a trip		
How the main character travels		
How the trip ends		

Name _____

Compare and Contrast Details

Think about sensory details that describe Chester's journey in *Chester Cricket's Pigeon Ride.* Then think about sensory details that describe a journey in another selection in this theme. Write the title of that selection on the line in the top right-hand box of the chart. Finally, write your details in the chart below. Fill as many rows as you can.

Selection Title	Chester Cricket's Pigeon Ride	_____
Sight		
Sound		
Taste		
Touch		
Smell		

Theme 1: **Journeys**   79

Name _____

Bridging Words

Match each word to its definition. Write the letter on the line beside the word. Then answer the questions below.

_____ **accompanying**   a. going along with

_____ **fare**   b. sorted into groups

_____ **parcel post**   c. very surprised

_____ **classified**   d. cost of a ticket

_____ **flabbergasted**   e. a kind of package delivery
                                      service

1. When would **parcel post** come in handy?

   _____

   _____

2. Why would it be helpful for a stamp collector to have her stamps **classified**?

   _____

   _____

3. When was a time that you felt **flabbergasted**?

   _____

   _____

4. How might a high **fare** make you feel about taking a trip?

   _____

   _____

5. Why is it a good idea to have guides **accompanying** museum visitors?

   _____

   _____

Name _____

Test Practice

Use the three steps you've learned to choose the best answer for these questions about *The Parcel Post Kid*. Fill in the circle for the best answer in the answer rows at the bottom of the page.

1. What was the author's purpose in writing *The Parcel Post Kid*?

   A to persuade parents not to mail their children

   B to tell a true story about an unusual trip

   C to explain how heavy packages were mailed in 1914

   D to tell about the time Leonard Mochel almost lost his job

2. Why do you think May's parents decided it was safe to mail her?

   F There had never been accident on the train to Grangeville.

   G Live animals were not allowed on the train.

   H Her cousin would be with her for the entire trip.

   J People were not allowed to mail poisons.

3. Why did the postmaster allow May to be mailed as a parcel?

   A Sending heavy objects by mail was a new idea at the time.

   B She passed the "smell test."

   C May was small and didn't weigh much.

   D The postmaster was May's cousin.

4. **Connecting/Comparing** Think about *The Parcel Post Kid* and *By the Shores of Silver Lake*. What did May carry on the train that Laura did not?

   F a ticket   **H** her baby sister

   G stamps and an address   **J** a suitcase

ANSWER ROWS   1 (A) (B) (C) (D)   3 (A) (B) (C) (D)

2 (F) (G) (H) (J)   4 (F) (G) (H) (J)

Continue on page 82.

Theme 1: **Journeys**   81

Name _____

Test Practice   continued

5. What happened because May went to get fresh air?

   A   The post office inspectors agreed to let Leonard keep his job.

   B   The train reached Granville on time.

   C   Mr. Morris told the newspapers about May's trip.

   D   May was classified as a baby chick.

6. Why do you think people were interested in a news story about May's trip to see her grandmother?

   F   Everyone was looking for a faster way of traveling than trains.

   G   Sending a child by parcel post sounded dangerous.

   H   It was a surprising idea.

   J   Leonard was famous for trying tricks on the railroad.

7. According to the post office inspectors, what rule should have been used when deciding whether to mail May?

   A   the rule that stopped people from sending live animals

   B   the rule that allowed people to send baby chicks

   C   the rule that stopped people from sending anything that smelled strongly

   D   the rule that allowed postal clerks to sort mail between towns

8. **Connecting/Comparing** In what way is Leonard Mochel like Lulu in *Chester Cricket's Pigeon Ride*?

   F   They both help someone save money.

   G   They both teach someone a history lesson.

   H   They both like to explore new places.

   J   They both take someone on an adventure.

ANSWER ROWS   5 (A) (B) (C) (D)   7 (A) (B) (C) (D)
              6 (F) (G) (H) (J)   8 (F) (G) (H) (J)

Name _____

The Author's Thoughts

Answer these questions about *The Parcel Post Kid.*

Which statement on page 134I indicates that the author thinks mailing a child by parcel post was unusual?

_____

_____

What are some of the words on page 134K that the author uses to describe the train ride?

_____

Based on these words, what is the author's opinion of the train ride?

_____

_____

Which words and details in the article show that the author thinks mailing May was "stretching the rules"?

_____

_____

Why do you think the author chose to write this article?

_____

_____

_____

 Theme 1: **Journeys**

Detail Chart

Complete this detail chart for *Chester Cricket's Pigeon Ride*.

Chester's Fall	**Important details about Chester's fall on page 134C** _____ _____ _____ _____ _____ _____
	Less important details about Chester's fall _____ _____
Lulu's Flight	**Important details about Lulu's flight on page 134E** _____ _____ _____ _____
	What do these details show what Lulu is feeling? _____ _____ _____

83

Journeys

Name _____

Syllabication

Syllables are the smaller parts you hear when you say a word aloud. For example, the word *postmaster* contains three syllables: post-mast-er. Some long words, such as *should*, have only one syllable.

Rewrite each word to show the syllables.

should
should (one)

announced
an-nounced (two)

packages
pack-ag-es (three)

1. parcel _____

2. granddaughter _____

3. would _____

4. seven _____

5. headline _____

6. ticket _____

7. surprises _____

8. something _____

9. laughed _____

10. because _____

11. wasted _____

12. adventure _____

Put Them in Order!

Put each group of words in alphabetical order. Write the words on the lines provided.

cricket   _____

chirp   _____

cling   _____

caught   _____

churning   _____

park   _____

pumped   _____

perch   _____

panting   _____

pupil   _____

drainpipe   _____

dizzy   _____

dip   _____

down   _____

deep   _____

Name _____

Spelling Review

**Write Spelling Words from the list on this page to
answer the questions.**

1–15. Which fifteen words have the /ă/ or /ā/ sound or
the /ĕ/ or /ē/ sound?

1. _____ 9. _____

2. _____ 10. _____

3. _____ 11. _____

4. _____ 12. _____

5. _____ 13. _____

6. _____ 14. _____

7. _____ 15. _____

8. _____

16–24. Which nine words have the /ĭ/ or /ī/ sound or the
/ŏ/ or /ō/ sound?

16. _____ 21. _____

17. _____ 22. _____

18. _____ 23. _____

19. _____ 24. _____

20. _____

25–30. Which six words have the /ŭ/, /yo͞o/, or /o͞o/ sound?

25. _____ 28. _____

26. _____ 29. _____

27. _____ 30. _____

Spelling Words

1. safe
2. few
3. tube
4. steep
5. past
6. steel
7. kept
8. gain
9. suit
10. steal
11. reach
12. sigh
13. wait
14. trunk
15. gray
16. still
17. coast
18. weight
19. grown
20. gold
21. odd
22. creek
23. wrote
24. crime
25. meat
26. blind
27. true
28. crumb
29. creak
30. meet

Name _____

Spelling Spree

Puzzle Play Write the Spelling Word that fits each clue.
Then use the letters in the boxes to write the secret word.
Begin the secret word with a capital letter.

1. did not throw out

2. unable to see

3. what toothpaste comes in

4. opposite of future

5. a large box for storage or travel

6. not moving

7. a tiny piece of food

Spelling Words
1. past
2. weight
3. kept
4. steel
5. creek
6. still
7. meat
8. blind
9. creak
10. steal
11. trunk
12. tube
13. crumb
14. wait
15. meet

Secret Word: _____

Hint: This famous ship struck an iceberg and sank on its first journey.

Homophone Hunt Write two Spelling Words that sound the same in each sentence.

8. We always _____ in the butcher shop to buy
_____ .

9. I can't _____ to find out my _____ !

10. In the breeze, the trees _____ near the shallow
_____ .

11. The robber tried to _____ the old
_____ safe.

Name _____

Proofreading and Writing

In the News Write the Spelling Word that completes each headline. Begin each word with a capital letter.

1. Man Rescues Cat and Breathes a _____
2. Many Leave Town But _____ Return
3. Miners Look for _____ Nearby
4. Dry Cleaner Loses Man's New _____
5. Two Climbers Lost on _____ Mountain
6. Schools _____ a Lot with New Plan
7. Lost Hiker Is Found _____ but Hungry
8. _____ Behavior in Skunks Signals Rabies
9. Two Arrested During _____ Spree

Spelling Words

1. reach
2. steep
3. gain
4. gold
5. gray
6. crime
7. coast
8. grown
9. odd
10. wrote
11. few
12. true
13. safe
14. suit
15. sigh

Proofreading Circle the six misspelled Spelling Words in this travel story. Then write each word correctly.

We left early and sailed along the coste. We hoped to reech the island in a few weeks, but it took a year. Some may think it strange that I never wroat about this journey before. Now my hair is graye, and my children are grone. At last, I can tell the trewe story.

10. _____   13. _____
11. _____   14. _____
12. _____   15. _____

✏ **Continue the Story** On a separate sheet of paper, write the rest of the story about the sailor's strange journey. Use the Spelling Review Words.

Name _____

Changing Sentences

Identify each sentence below as a statement, a command, a question, or an exclamation. Then rewrite it as the kind of sentence described on the next line.

1. Could you drop me off in Times Square? _____
   (command) _____

2. It costs 53 cents to send a package to Lewiston. _____
   (question) _____

3. You can see a lot from the top of the Empire State Building. _____
   (exclamation) _____

4. Take me to my grandmother's house. _____
   (statement) _____

5. How strange it must feel to be mailed! _____
   (question) _____

Name _____

Identifying Subjects and Predicates

In each sentence, mark a line between the complete subject and the complete predicate. Then write the complete subject and the complete predicate on the lines provided.

1. The black cricket chirped happily.

   Subject: _____

   Predicate: _____

2. A gust of wind blew my hat out of my hand.

   Subject: _____

   Predicate: _____

3. The young girl rode the train through the mountains.

   Subject: _____

   Predicate: _____

4. That man in the dark blue coat works in the Post Office.

   Subject: _____

   Predicate: _____

5. Three gray pigeons strutted around the statue.

   Subject: _____

   Predicate: _____

Name _____

The Missing Words Mystery

Write the word that completes each sentence. Then solve the riddle.

1. A __ __ __ __ can help solve a mystery.
   ₆

2. The __ __ __ __ __ __ __ saw everything that
   ₃
   happened.

3. A __ __ __ __ is something that is being investigated.
   ₉

4. Will you catch the __ __ __ __ __ __ __ __ who
   ₂
   committed this crime?

5. She is a __ __ __ __ __ __ __, but I am not sure if she is guilty.
   ₅

6. The __ __ __ __ __ __ __ __ __ tried to find out what really
   ₄   ₁
   happened.

7. When you have all of the __ __ __ __ __ __ __ __, you can draw a
   ₁₀
   conclusion.

8. The answer to a mystery is the __ __ __ __ __ __ __ __.
   ₇

9. The case has a lot of __ __ __ __ __ __ __ __ because the ending is
   ₈
   uncertain.

Vocabulary

- case
- clue
- criminal
- detective
- evidence
- solution
- suspect
- suspense
- witness

What do detectives say when they solve a crime?

___ ___ ___ ___   ___ ___ ___ ___ ___ ___
1 2 3 4   5 6 7 8 9 10

Name _____

Story Map: "The Case of the Earthenware Pig"

Characters
Detective: _____   Other Characters: Suspect(s): _____   _____

Setting: _____

Mystery: _____

Events/Plot: _____

_____

_____

_____

Evidence or Clues:	Solution:
_____	_____
_____	_____
_____	_____
_____	_____
_____	_____
_____	_____

Name _____

The Perfect Detective

Think about the two detectives you have read about in *Focus on Mysteries*. **Use the chart below to describe their characteristics. Then list which characteristics you think the perfect detective would have. How do Encyclopedia Brown and the Judge compare to your perfect detective?**

Encyclopedia Brown	**The Judge**
1. smart	1. smart
2. _____	2. _____
3. _____	3. _____
4. _____	4. _____

The Perfect Detective

1. _____
2. _____
3. _____
4. _____

How the Detectives Compare

1. _____
2. _____
3. _____
4. _____

Name _____

The Interview

Imagine that you are interviewing Encyclopedia Brown for your school newspaper. You want to show that someone Encyclopedia Brown's age can be a good detective. List the questions you would ask him. Then act out your interview with a friend.

1. _____
_____
_____

2. _____
_____
_____

3. _____
_____
_____

4. _____
_____

Name _____

Story Map: "The Sticks of Truth"

Characters

Detective: _____

Suspect(s): _____

Other Characters:

_____

_____

Setting: _____

Mystery: _____

Events/Plot: _____

_____

_____

_____

_____

Trick:

_____

_____

_____

_____

_____

_____

Solution:

_____

_____

_____

_____

_____

_____

Name _____

What Happened to Sam?

You can add *-ed* or *-ing* endings to some base words.

look   look**ed**   look**ing**

You can add *-er* or *-est* endings to some base words.

old   old**er**   old**est**

When a base word ends in *e*, the *e* is dropped before *-ed* or *-ing*
is added. It is also dropped before the endings *-er* and *-est*.

stare   star**ed**   star**ing**

safe   saf**er**   saf**est**

**Read the story below. Circle each word with an *-ed*
or *-ing* ending. Circle each word with an *-er* or *-est*
ending. Then write the base words in the box.**

Base Words
1. _____
2. _____
3. _____
4. _____
5. _____
6. _____
7. _____
8. _____
9. _____
10. _____
11. _____
12. _____
13. _____
14. _____
15. _____

The sun is shining, but Sam has disappeared.

Yesterday, Sam watched proudly from his favorite
place. He loved standing in the middle of the lawn.
The coldest wind of the season blasted his face. Heavy
snow was falling, but Sam kept smiling.

Today, a gentler breeze is blowing. Now the
temperature is growing warmer. Some people are
taking off their coats.

But Sam is missing.

Can you solve this mystery? The answer is upside-
down below.

Sam was a snowman.

Name _____

More Short and Long Vowels

Remember that a short vowel sound is usually spelled by the vowel letter and is followed by a consonant sound.

/ă/ pl**a**nt   /ĕ/ d**e**sk   /ĭ/ f**i**st   /ŏ/ bl**o**ck   /ŭ/ tr**u**ck

Remember these spelling patterns for long vowel sounds.

/ā/ sh**a**ke, spr**ay**, dr**ai**n   /ē/ n**ea**t, sp**ee**d   /ī/ pr**ide**, fr**igh**t

/ō/ r**oa**st, c**o**n**e**   /o͞o/ pr**u**n**e**, cr**ew**

Write each Spelling Word under its vowel sound.
Underline the pattern that spells the vowel sound.

1. shake
2. desk
3. block
4. fright
5. neat
6. roast
7. prune
8. spray
9. plant
10. bread*
11. speed
12. drain
13. fist
14. pride
15. truck
16. flock
17. cone
18. crew
19. blade
20. dead*

/ē/ Sound	/ī/ Sound
_____	_____
_____	_____

/ō/ Sound	/yo͞o/ or /o͞o/ Sound
_____	_____
_____	_____

/ā/ Sound

_____   _____

_____   _____

Short Vowel Sounds

_____   _____

_____   _____

_____   _____

_____   _____

Name _____

Spelling Spree

Mystery Titles Write the Spelling Word that best completes each title for a mystery. Begin each word with a capital letter.

1. *The Case of the Missing Birdwatcher and the _____ of Geese.*

2. *The Case of the Swordsman and the Broken _____*

3. *The Case of the Bad Pet-Sitter and the _____ Goldfish*

4. *The Case of the Leaky _____*

5. *The Case of the Too _____ Closet*

6. *The Case of the Stolen Sailboat and Its Singing _____*

7. *The Case of the Driver Who Broke the _____ Limit*

The Third Word Write the Spelling Word that best fits with each pair of words.

8. chart, lamp, _____

9. square, triangle, _____

10. apple, pear, _____

11. boil, fry, _____

12. finger, thumb, _____

13. toy, game, _____

14. stream, drizzle, _____

15. flower, tree, _____

Name _____

Proofreading and Writing

Proofreading Circle the five misspelled Spelling Words
in this beginning to a detective story. Then write each
word correctly.

I had just begun watering the plant on my desk.
Suddenly a man raced into my office at top speed.

"You have to help me!" he cried.

"Slow down," I said. "You must have had a bad frite."

"You are right," he answered, starting to shaik. "My truk
has been stolen, and I need to get it back right away. It's full
of bred for a big party."

"You've come to the right place," I said with prid. "I can
solve this mystery."

1. _____   4. _____

2. _____   5. _____

3. _____

Spelling Words

1. shake
2. desk
3. block
4. fright
5. neat
6. roast
7. prune
8. spray
9. plant
10. bread*
11. speed
12. drain
13. fist
14. pride
15. truck
16. flock
17. cone
18. crew
19. blade
20. dead*

➤ **Write a Description** A jewelry store has been
robbed, and you have been asked to investigate the crime.

**On a separate sheet of paper, write a description of the
crime scene. Include clues that give an idea of what
happened and how. Use Spelling Words from the list.**

Name _____

Mystery Idioms

Read the following passage. Then write the letter of the correct meaning in the blank next to each idiom.

"Have you seen Mark lately? He's been acting odd," George said.

"What do you mean?" I asked. "Do you think Mark's <u>up to something</u> again? He's always playing tricks on people."

"That's just it. He's had a <u>long face</u> all week. He hasn't smiled or laughed once," George said. "In fact, I asked him to help me trick you, and he didn't get excited at all. It's like he <u>doesn't have his heart in it</u>."

"You're right, that is odd. Do you suppose he's still feeling <u>under the weather</u>? He was sick last week," I suggested.

"I don't know. I asked him what's <u>bugging</u> him, but he won't tell me what's wrong. He just <u>clams up</u>. He won't say a word."

"That's really odd!" I said. "Let's get Mark and <u>get to the bottom of</u> this! We'll find out the truth!"

	Idiom		Meaning
1. _____	up to something	a.	bothering
2. _____	long face	b.	learn why it happened
3. _____	doesn't have his heart in it	c.	planning; scheming
4. _____	under the weather	d.	sad expression
5. _____	bugging	e.	refuses to talk
6. _____	clams up	f.	sick
7. _____	get to the bottom of	g.	isn't enthusiastic

Name _____

Which or Where?

Read the following passage. Underline each phrase that tells *which* **or** *where.* **Then complete the sentence that the dog is thinking, using a phrase that tells** *where.*

Good morning, Detective Jiménez. I'm glad I found you at home. My name is Fred, and I live down the street. Can you help me find my glasses? I've spent all day searching around my house. I thought I left them in the drawer of the table, but they weren't there. So then I looked under the table and behind the dresser, but they weren't there either. Next, I searched through the clothes in my closet and among my shoes. Finally, I gave up. I think it's really strange that my glasses are missing. I was wearing them as I read my book about forgetfulness last night, just before I fell asleep in bed.

Fred, your glasses are

_____.

Name _____

Adding Phrases

Rewrite each sentence, adding a phrase that tells *which* or *where*.

1. Did you ever meet Detective Brown?

   _____

2. Is he famous?

   _____

3. Yes, he solved a case recently.

   _____

4. Will you take me to meet him?

   _____

5. He might be able to help me find the lost presents.

   _____

6. Detective Brown can find missing items anywhere.

   _____

Name _____

Sentence Variety

**Rewrite the following paragraph, changing two sentence types
and adding five phrases that tell *which* or *where*.**

There's a famous detective at Lincoln Elementary
School. All her friends call her Detective. Her parents
call her Ruth. She found her teacher's missing keys.
She also discovered several lost scarves and mittens.
Ruth has a gift. She may start her own business.

_____

_____

_____

_____

_____

Name _____

You're the Author

Write down ideas and details to include in your mystery. Put a star next to the events where you will give clues.

Characters	
Detective: _____	Other Characters:
Suspect(s): _____	_____
_____	_____

Mystery: _____
_____

Setting: _____
_____

Events/Plot (slip in clues): _____
_____
_____
_____
_____
_____
_____
_____
_____

Solution: _____
_____

Name _____

Using Time-Order Words

Read the following passage. Then fill in each blank with the word from the box that makes the most sense. Use each word once.

Time-Order Words	
then	after
next	before
early	when
finally	morning
now	first

The Great Muffin Mystery

"Who stole all my muffins?" yelled my brother. "Show yourself, thief!" The dog, my sister, and I trooped into the kitchen to see what all the fuss was about. The cat was nowhere to be found.

My brother glared _____ at my sister, _____ at me, and _____ at the dog. The dog looked away. My sister said, "_____ you blame anyone, could you please tell us what you're talking about?"

My brother explained, "_____ this _____, I baked muffins for breakfast. _____ they were done, I put them on the table to cool and left the kitchen. And _____ the tray holds only crumbs!"

Just _____ we heard a small hiccup from under the kitchen table. We all turned to look. There lay our fat family cat, with crumbs all over her face. _____ my sister saw her, she asked with a grin, "Would you care to guess who ate your muffins?"

Name _____

Tell About America

You are visiting another country and meet someone your age. Your new friend wants to know about the United States, and asks you the questions below. Help your friend learn about the United States by answering these questions.

1. What kind of food do people in the United States like to eat?

_____

2. What is an American school like?

_____

3. What do you and your friends like to do on weekends?

_____

Think of another question your friend might ask. Write an answer to it.

_____

_____

_____

_____

Name _____

New Places

	Who is the story about? Where do they go in the story?	How are the characters' lives changed by going to the new place?
Tomás and the Library Lady		
Tanya's Reunion		
Boss of the Plains		
A Very Important Day		

Name _____

Let's Read

Vocabulary

borrow   check out   eager   glaring   storyteller   lap

Choose the best meaning for the underlined word.
Write the letter of your answer on the line provided.

1. Many people <u>borrow</u> books and records from libraries. _____
   A. use for a short time   B. lend   C. dig a hole for   D. steal

2. I would like to <u>check out</u> that book for two weeks. _____
   A. pay the bill for   B. borrow   C. prove true   D. add up

3. I am very <u>eager</u> to read the book you gave me for my birthday. _____
   A. careful   B. uninterested   C. demanding   D. interested

4. The old house near the bus stop, with its broken windows
   <u>glaring</u> down at us, can be scary. _____
   A. obvious   B. dark   C. sharp   D. to stare in an
                                                          angry way

5. Stories always seem better when read aloud by a good <u>storyteller</u>. _____
   A. person who   B. liar   C. actor   D. speaker
      tells stories

6. After school I will read, and my cat will quietly <u>lap</u> up her milk. _____
   A. spill   B. lick up   C. pour   D. share

Name _____

Event Map

Pages 160–161

At midnight, the family was headed by car _____
_____

Pages 162–165

The boys carried water to the field, and when they got hot, they _____
_____

Pages 166–167

First the library lady took Tomás to a drinking fountain. Then she _____
_____

Pages 168–170

All summer, whenever he could, Tomás _____
_____

Pages 171–174

In the evenings, Tomás _____
_____

Name _____

Check Your Memory

Think about the selection. Then complete the sentences.

1. The Rivera family traveled to Iowa each summer because _____
   _____
   _____

2. Tomás wanted to learn new stories so he could _____
   _____
   _____

3. Tomás was able to forget about both Iowa and Texas when _____
   _____
   _____

4. Tomás got a small sample of what it's like to be a teacher when _____
   _____
   _____

5. Tomás was sad to say the word *adiós* because _____
   _____
   _____
   _____

Name _____

A Summer Sequence

Read the story below and answer the questions on the following page.

Audrey's Dream

It was a late summer afternoon. Sitting in the shade not far from her friend Sharon, Audrey looked through the book her father had loaned her. The book was all about the world of dinosaurs. In the heat, Audrey felt sleepy.

As she read, Audrey seemed to see real dinosaurs standing by a pond and drinking cool water. Even though her eyes were closing, Audrey seemed to hear the cry of the wild snakebird. A minute later, she was on the back of a dinosaur. She felt its warm neck as she held on tight.

The dinosaur carried Audrey across fields and swamps and into forests. Together they traveled many miles toward the setting sun. At last they ended up on a grassy plain. All was still. Audrey could hear nothing, but the dinosaur was listening for something that only it could hear.

Then in the distance, Audrey saw a shadow. A moment later, she saw a huge, fierce dinosaur she recognized from the book. The dinosaur she was riding began to run.

Faster and faster it ran across the plain. Looking behind her, Audrey saw huge teeth and claws getting closer and closer. Just then she heard a loud thud.

"Audrey, wake up!" she heard Sharon say. "You fell asleep. What would your father say if he knew you let his book fall in the dirt?"

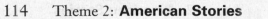

Name _____

A Summer Sequence continued

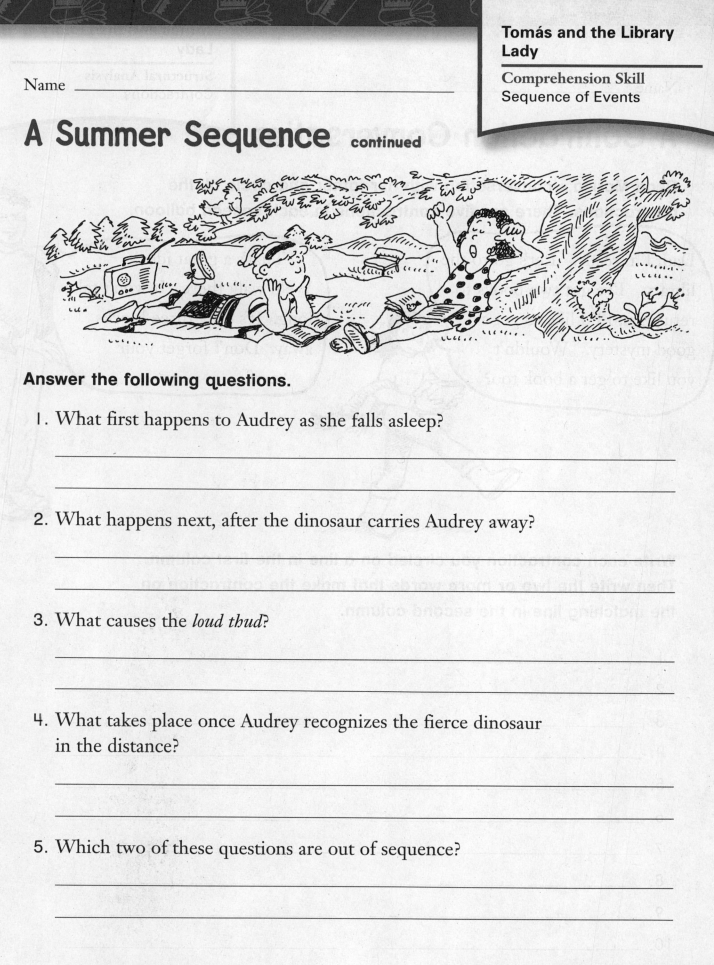

Answer the following questions.

1. What first happens to Audrey as she falls asleep?

_____

_____

2. What happens next, after the dinosaur carries Audrey away?

_____

_____

3. What causes the *loud thud*?

_____

_____

4. What takes place once Audrey recognizes the fierce dinosaur in the distance?

_____

_____

5. Which two of these questions are out of sequence?

_____

_____

Name _____

A Contraction Conversation

Read Marisa's conversation with her father and circle all the contractions. There are five contractions in each speech balloon.

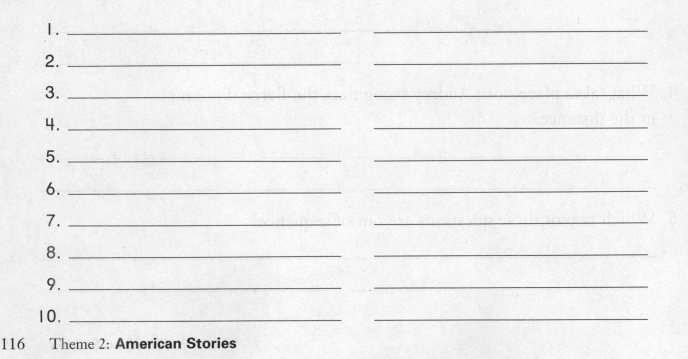

Dad, I'm ready. Let's go to the library. I've got two books to return, and I'd like to get a good mystery. Wouldn't you like to get a book too?

That's a great idea! We'll walk there. It won't take long. It's only three blocks away. Don't forget your scarf.

Write each contraction you circled on a line in the first column. Then write the two or more words that make the contraction on the matching line in the second column.

1. _____ _____
2. _____ _____
3. _____ _____
4. _____ _____
5. _____ _____
6. _____ _____
7. _____ _____
8. _____ _____
9. _____ _____
10. _____ _____

Name _____

The /ou/ and /ô/ Sounds

When you hear the /ou/ or the /ô/ sound, think of these patterns:

> /ou/ *ou* or *ow*   /ô/ *aw, au,* or *a* before *l*

Remember that a consonant sound usually follows the *ou* or the *au* pattern.

> /ou/ p**ou**nd, h**ow**l   /ô/ j**aw**, c**au**se, **a**lways

► In the starred word, *couple, ou* spells the /ŭ/ sound, not the /ou/ sound.

Write each Spelling Word under its vowel sound.

/ou/ Sound	/ô/ Sound
_____	_____
_____	_____
_____	_____
_____	_____
_____	_____
_____	_____
_____	_____
_____	**Another Vowel Sound**
_____	_____
_____	_____
_____	

Spelling Words

1. pound
2. howl
3. jaw
4. bounce
5. cause
6. always
7. shout
8. aloud
9. south
10. couple*
11. drawn
12. scout
13. false
14. proud
15. frown
16. sauce
17. gown
18. couch
19. dawn
20. mount

Name _____

Spelling Spree

Letter Swap Change the first letter of each word to make a Spelling Word. Write the word.

Example: talk   *walk*

1. sound   _____

2. down   _____

3. brown   _____

4. law   _____

Puzzle Play Write a Spelling Word to fit each clue.

Example: a joking performer who does tricks

c l o (w) n

5. filled with pride

6. a pair

7. a liquid topping for food

8. attracted; sketched

9. to explore for information

10. to cry out

11. to climb or get up on

12. to move with a bobbing motion

Now write the circled letters in order. They spell three words Papá Grande often said to Tomás.

☐ ☐ ☐ ☐   ☐ ☐   ☐ ☐ .

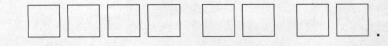

Name _____

Proofreading and Writing

Proofreading Suppose Tomás sent a postcard to a friend. Circle the five misspelled Spelling Words in this postcard. Then write each word correctly.

Dear Antonio,

After a couple of fallse starts, we finally got on the road last Friday. It is sure a long way from the sowth up to Iowa! We hope to arrive by daun tomorrow. Papá Grande's stories have been making us houl with laughter. He allways makes the trips go faster!

Your friend,

Tomás

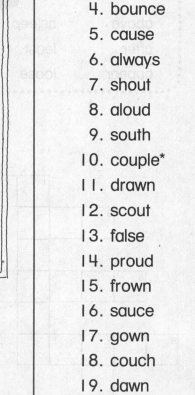

Spelling Words

1. pound
2. howl
3. jaw
4. bounce
5. cause
6. always
7. shout
8. aloud
9. south
10. couple*
11. drawn
12. scout
13. false
14. proud
15. frown
16. sauce
17. gown
18. couch
19. dawn
20. mount

1. _____
2. _____
3. _____
4. _____
5. _____

✏️ **Write a Description** Tomás and his family often made the trip between Texas and Iowa. Have you taken an interesting trip? Did you travel by car, bus, train, or plane? What did you see and do?

On a separate sheet of paper, write a description of a trip you have taken. Use Spelling Words from the list.

Name _____

Antonym Puzzle

Complete the crossword puzzle by writing the correct antonym for each clue. Choose your answers from the words in the box. Remember, an antonym is a word that means the opposite or nearly the opposite of another word.

Vocabulary

above	asleep	lost	start	true
after	least	push	sunny	winter
appear	loose	raise	top	return

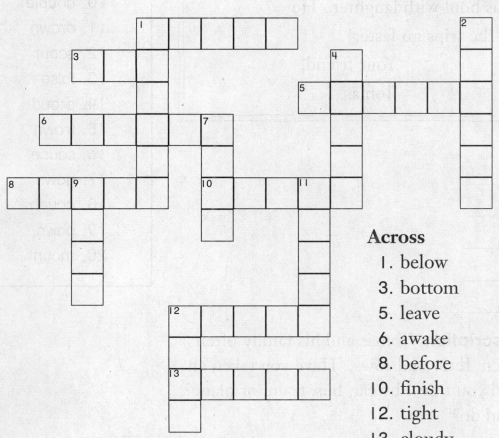

Across
1. below
3. bottom
5. leave
6. awake
8. before
10. finish
12. tight
13. cloudy

Down
1. vanish
2. summer
4. most
7. pull
9. false
11. lower
12. found

Finding Proper Nouns

Underline the proper nouns in each sentence.

1. As a boy, Tomás Rivera traveled with his parents.
2. The Rivera family came to the United States from Mexico.
3. The family picked crops in Texas and in Iowa.
4. The young boy called his parents Mamá and Papá.
5. The boy's grandfather told stories to him and his brother, Enrique, in Spanish.
6. The boy sometimes told stories to Papá Grande in English.
7. The boy grew up to become a famous Mexican American.
8. A beautiful library in Riverside, California, is named for him.

Write each underlined proper noun in the correct space below.

Person	Place	Thing

Completing with Proper Nouns

**Complete each sentence with a proper noun from
*Tomás and the Library Lady.***

1. Tomás's family is driving to the state of _____.

2. Tomás calls his grandfather _____.

3. Tomás's brother's name is _____.

4. Their grandfather tells stories in _____.

5. The _____
   is in Denton, Texas.

**Write a proper noun for each person, place, or thing
described.**

6. the first and last name of a friend or relative _____

   _____

7. the state where you live _____

   _____

8. a language you speak _____

   _____

9. your favorite book or movie _____

   _____

10. the name of your school or library _____

   _____

Writing Proper Nouns

Name _____

Proofread the paragraph below. Find common nouns that have capital letters. Find proper nouns that need capital letters. Use the proofreading marks to show the corrections. Then write the corrected common and proper nouns in the columns below.

Proofreading Marks

Make a small letter: S̸tory

Make a capital letter: mexico

The Woman who wrote the story is pat mora. She was born in El Paso, texas. The Illustrator is Raul colón. He is an Artist from puerto rico. The story is about a young Boy named tomás rivera. He learns to love Books from the kind library lady. He grew up to become a famous mexican american.

Common Nouns	**Proper Nouns**
_____	_____
_____	_____
_____	_____
_____	_____
_____	_____
_____	_____

Name _____

Writing an Essay

Use this page to help you plan your essay. Write your focus idea first. Then write two reasons or facts about your topic in the boxes below. Finally, think of some examples you could use to make each reason or fact clear.

My Focus Idea

_____

_____

_____

_____

_____

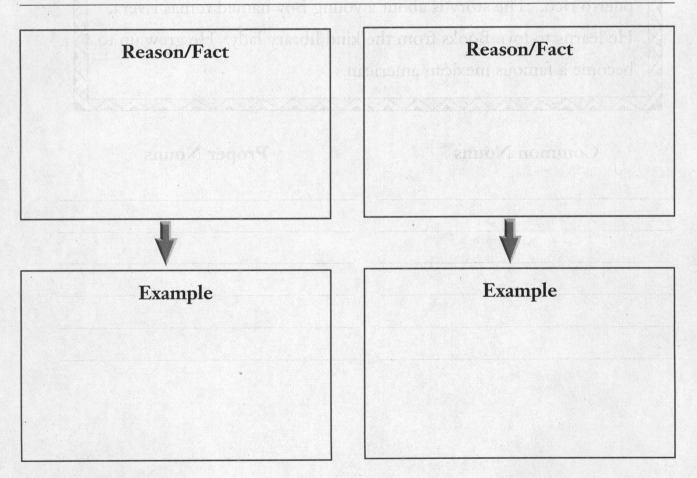

Reason/Fact	**Reason/Fact**

Example	**Example**

Name _____

Improving Your Writing

Read the following essay. Then add reasons to the main idea of paragraphs 2, 3 and 4 that support that idea. Write your reasons on the lines provided.

Afternoons at the Library

One afternoon a week, I usually stop by our local public library. Each time I go, I try to find at least one book that I want to read. Sometimes I find a new book of stories. Sometimes I discover an exciting mystery novel. Sometimes I find a nonfiction book about science or history.

Stories always appeal to me.

Add two or three sentences that give possible reasons why stories are appealing.

_____

_____

_____

I have to admit that mystery novels get my attention, too.

Add two or three sentences that give possible reasons why mystery novels might be interesting to read.

_____

_____

_____

Books about science and history are my favorite kinds of nonfiction.

Add two or three sentences that give reasons why science or history might be appealing choices for a reader.

_____

_____

_____

Revising Your Description

Reread your description. Put a checkmark in the box for each sentence that describes your paper. Use this page to help you revise.

Rings the Bell

☐ The beginning clearly tells what the description is about.

☐ Details tell what I saw, heard, smelled, tasted or felt. They are clearly ordered.

☐ My writing sounds like me.

☐ Sensory words create vivid pictures.

☐ Sentences flow smoothly, and there are few mistakes.

Getting Stronger

☐ The beginning could be more clear.

☐ I need more details. I could order them more clearly.

☐ My voice could be stronger.

☐ I could add more sensory words.

☐ The sentences don't always flow smoothly, and there are some mistakes.

Try Harder

☐ The beginning is not clear.

☐ There are few details. The order is confusing.

☐ I can't hear my voice at all.

☐ There are no sensory words.

☐ Most sentences are choppy. There are many mistakes.

Sentence Combining

Combine each pair of sentences into one sentence. Write a new sentence that has a compound subject or compound predicate, or write a compound sentence. Use the joining word in parentheses. Add commas where they are needed.

1. Mary fed the cat.
2. Ben fed the cat. (or)

_____

3. The cat sat on my favorite chair.
4. The cat took a nap. (and)

_____

5. The dog held a bone in its paws.
6. The dog chewed on it. (and)

_____

_____

7. The kitten knocked over the lamp.
8. The puppy knocked over the lamp. (or)

_____

_____

9. The kitten watched the raindrops through the window.
10. The puppy barked at the thunder. (but)

_____

_____

11. The kitten snuggled up next to the puppy.
12. Soon both animals were fast asleep. (and)

_____

_____

Name _____

Spelling Words

Words Often Misspelled Look for familiar spelling to help you remember how to spell the Spelling Words on this page. Think carefully about the parts that you find hard to spell in each word.

Write the missing letters in the Spelling Words below.

1. a _____ _____ _____

2. oth _____ _____

3. _____ _____ other

4. _____ nyone

5. ev _____ ry

6. som _____ one

7. mys _____ _____ _____

8. fam _____ ly

9. fr _____ _____ nd

10. p _____ ple

11. _____ g _____ _____ n

12. _____ nything

13. _____ nyway

14. ev _____ _____ yone

15. f _____ rst

Spelling Words
1. a lot
2. other
3. another
4. anyone
5. every
6. someone
7. myself
8. family
9. friend
10. people
11. again
12. anything
13. anyway
14. everyone
15. first

Study List On a separate piece of paper, write each Spelling Word. Check your spelling against the words on the list.

Name _____

Spelling Spree

Sentence Fillers Write the Spelling Word that best completes each sentence.

1. Did you ever find your _____ glove?

2. I'd like you to meet my best _____ , Philip.

3. My sister got _____ question on her math test right.

4. Can we get you _____ from the store?

5. It was hard to get _____ to agree on a movie.

6. Next summer, we're visiting my mom's _____ out west.

7. I'm getting _____ piece of pizza.

8. I think that _____ called our house late last night.

Spelling Words

1. a lot
2. other
3. another
4. anyone
5. every
6. someone
7. myself
8. family
9. friend
10. people
11. again
12. anything
13. anyway
14. everyone
15. first

Word Clues Write a Spelling Word to fit each clue.

9. a word meaning "just the same" _____

10. one more time _____

11. a synonym for anybody _____

12. a crowd of human beings _____

13. coming before anything else _____

14. the opposite of a little _____

15. a word you use when talking about you _____

I'll do it <u>myself</u>!

Theme 2: **American Stories** 129

Proofreading and Writing

Proofreading Circle the five misspelled Spelling Words in this speech. Then write each word correctly.

1. a lot
2. other
3. another
4. anyone
5. every
6. someone
7. myself
8. family
9. friend
10. people
11. again
12. anything
13. anyway
14. everyone
15. first

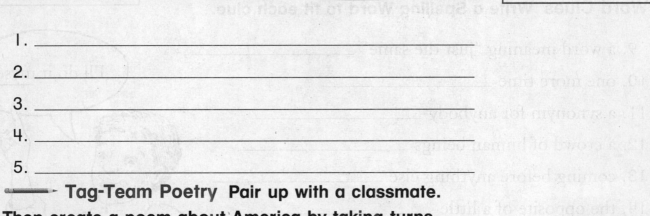

If somone were to ask you, "What is an American?" what would you say? I think that evryone has his or her own answer. But when I ask myslef this question, my first answer is "a person who believes in democracy." It is democracy that lets each one of the American peple have a say in the direction of our country. If there is anythin more important to being an American, I can't think of it.

1. _____
2. _____
3. _____
4. _____
5. _____

Tag-Team Poetry Pair up with a classmate. Then create a poem about America by taking turns writing lines. Use Spelling Words from the list.

Name _____

Name _____

A Family Get-Together

Aunt Sally had to miss the big family party. Kara writes to tell her all about it. Complete Kara's letter by filling in the blank with the correct word from the list.

Dear Aunt Sally,

    I am sorry that you missed the family

_____. We all had great fun, and

saw many relatives from both near and far away. Nearly

sixty people came for the party. It was the largest family

_____ in years. There were

many familiar faces, and a few I didn't know at all. Two

great-aunts and one _____ came

all the way from Oregon. My dad made the travel

_____ for them. They had not

seen our house for twenty years. They called our house and

the surrounding land the _____.

    One of the things that I like is that everyone

_____ to prepare food. It's too

much work for just a few people. I got a great deal of

_____ from seeing how many of

the relatives liked my potato salad. The only thing wrong

with the day was that the bees _____

in buzzing around the desserts.

    I hope you can come visit soon.

                      Yours truly,
                      Your niece Kara

Vocabulary

arrangements
gathering
great-uncle
homestead
persisted
pitches in
reunion
satisfaction

Theme 2: **American Stories**

Name _____

Character Development Flow Chart

Story Event or Character Detail	+	My Own Experience	=	Inference About Character
page 189 When Grandma says she's leaving for the reunion without Tanya and the family, silence falls across the dinner table.	+	I know that _____ _____ _____ _____	=	I can infer that _____ _____ _____ _____
page 196 When Tanya gets to the farm, she doesn't find what she expects.	+	I know that _____ _____ _____	=	I can infer that _____ _____ _____
page 196 When Aunt Kay hugs Tanya, the warm, soft hug reminds Tanya of Grandma.	+	I know that _____ _____ _____	=	I can infer that _____ _____ _____
200 Tanya stops looks closely at the "memories" in ng parlor.	+	I know that _____ _____ _____ _____ _____	=	I can infer that _____ _____ _____ _____

131

American Stories

Name _____

Just the Facts

Complete the following to show the setting, major events, and the ending for *Tanya's Reunion*.

Setting:
_____
_____
_____
_____

Events:
_____
_____
_____
_____
_____
_____
_____
_____
_____
_____

Ending:
_____
_____
_____
_____

Name _____

What Characters!

Read the story below. Then complete the chart on the following page.

Family Tree

"Let's make a family tree!" said Meghan. "We can look for family records on the Internet."

"We could never do that," said her brother Brian, shaking his head. "The Internet is too huge."

"Nonsense," said Meghan. "We know that some of our great-grandparents lived in Lowell, Massachusetts. Using the Internet, we can scan the Lowell city records for other information."

A few computer clicks later, Meghan and Brian found the city's records. "Look, there they are!" said Meghan, her hands trembling. "Bridget and James O'Toole were married in Lowell on June 11, 1896. It says her parents were Sean and Maeve Boyle. His parents were James and Rose O'Toole."

"Can we tell where they were born?" asked Brian.

"Maybe," said Meghan. "Here are passenger lists for ships arriving in Boston in the 1880s and 1890s. Let's check to see if we can find their names."

"Look!" said Brian, staring wide-eyed at the computer screen. "Here are James and Rose O'Toole listed as passengers on the *Adelaide* that sailed in 1888 from Ireland."

Meghan sighed. "That means that if we want more information, we'll have to look for records in Ireland!"

Name _____

What Characters! continued

Use the story and your own experiences to complete the following chart.

Story Event	+	My Own Experience	=	Inference About Character
Brian shakes his head when Meghan suggests searching the Internet.	+	I may shake my head _____ _____ _____	=	I can infer that _____ _____ _____ _____
Meghan's hands tremble when she finds the family records.	+	My hands may tremble _____ _____ _____	=	I can infer that _____ _____ _____ _____
Brian stares wide-eyed at the computer screen.	+	I may stare wide-eyed _____ _____ _____	=	I can infer that _____ _____ _____ _____
Meghan sighs when she learns that their search must extend to Ireland.	+	I may sigh _____ _____ _____ _____	=	I can infer that _____ _____ _____ _____

Name _____

Root It Out

The word root *sign* means "a sign or mark."
The word root *spect* means "to look at."

    Example: The **spectators** cheered loudly.

    The runners waited for the **signal** to start the race.

**Use the words in the box to complete the story. If you
need help, use a dictionary.**

signaled	suspected	inspect	signified	spectacular
respect	signature	spectacles	designs	expected

    When Jenna woke up, she knew the raindrops hitting her

window _____ another day inside. Jenna

decided to _____ the dusty attic. A lot

of the items she found looked like junk, but Jenna knew each item

_____ an important part of her family's

history and deserved _____. Jenna loved

the colorful _____ on the old quilts.

They were _____! Next she tried

looking through _____ that she

_____ belonged to her grandmother long

ago. Then Tanya read some letters that had her great-grandfather's

_____. She hadn't

_____ to find that!

Name _____

The /o͞o/ and /o͝o/ Sounds

When you hear the /o͞o/ sound, think of the pattern *oo*. Remember that the /o͝o/ sound is often spelled *oo* or *u* followed by a consonant or a cluster.

/o͞o/ t**oo**l /o͝o/ w**oo**d, p**u**t

▶ The starred words *group*, *prove*, *soup*, and *move* use different spelling patterns for the /o͞o/ sound.

Write each Spelling Word under its vowel sound. Include *roof* **with the /o͞o/ sound.**

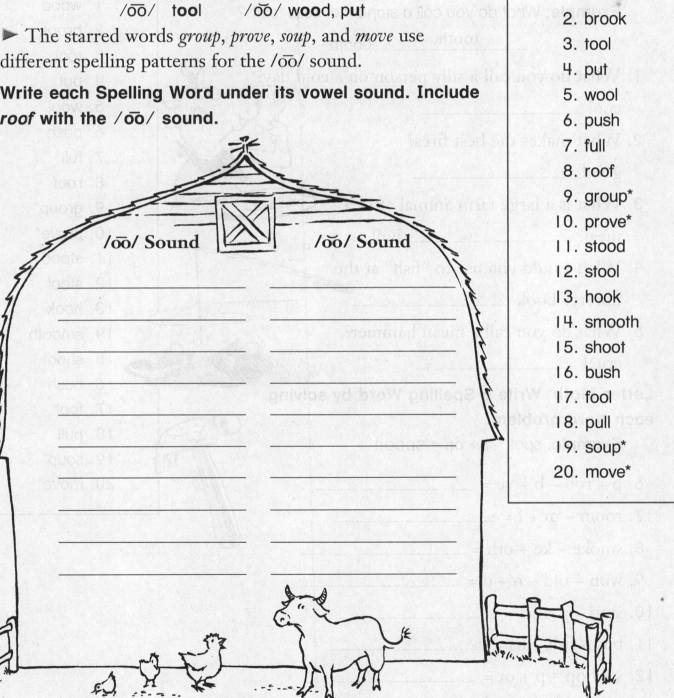

/o͞o/ Sound   /o͝o/ Sound

Spelling Words

1. wood
2. brook
3. tool
4. put
5. wool
6. push
7. full
8. roof
9. group*
10. prove*
11. stood
12. stool
13. hook
14. smooth
15. shoot
16. bush
17. fool
18. pull
19. soup*
20. move*

Name _____

Spelling Spree

Hink Pinks Write a Spelling Word that answers the question and rhymes with the given word.

Example: What do you call a stand that sells teeth?

_____tooth_____ booth

1. What do you call a silly person on a cold day?

cool _____

2. What makes the best fires?

good _____

3. What is a large farm animal after a

meal? _____ bull

4. What would you use to "fish" at the

library? book _____

5. What do you call a mean hammer?

cruel _____

Letter Math Write a Spelling Word by solving each word problem.

Example: spot − t + on = spoon

6. p + rob − b + ve = _____

7. room − m + f = _____

8. smoke − ke + oth = _____

9. won + old − n − d = _____

10. stop − p + od = _____

11. bus + fish − fis = _____

12. s + hop − p + ot = _____

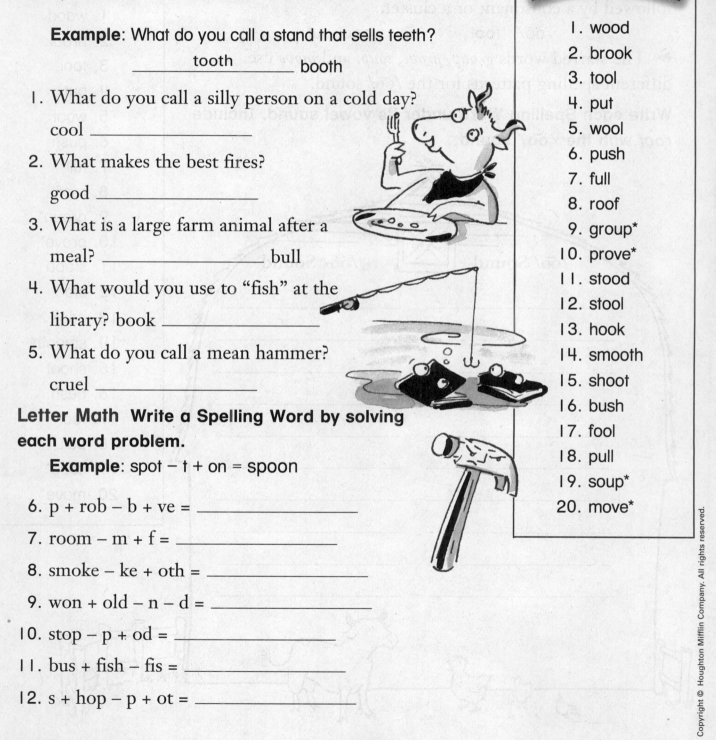

Spelling Words

1. wood
2. brook
3. tool
4. put
5. wool
6. push
7. full
8. roof
9. group*
10. prove*
11. stood
12. stool
13. hook
14. smooth
15. shoot
16. bush
17. fool
18. pull
19. soup*
20. move*

Name _____

Proofreading and Writing

Proofreading Circle the five misspelled Spelling Words in this diary entry. Then write each word correctly on the lines below.

Spelling Words

1. wood
2. brook
3. tool
4. put
5. wool
6. push
7. full
8. roof
9. group*
10. prove*
11. stood
12. stool
13. hook
14. smooth
15. shoot
16. bush
17. fool
18. pull
19. soup*
20. move*

Today a groop of us made taffy for the reunion. After cooking it, we putt it on a counter. One person's job was to poush the blob of taffy down. Then two others picked it up. Their job was to pul the blob to stretch it. This helped to make the taffy smooth. We did this over and over. It was hard work! Tonight I am so sore I can hardly mouve.

_____

_____

_____

_____

Write a Recipe What food dish would you like to take to a family reunion?

On a separate piece of paper, write a recipe for a dish that you might make. List what is in the dish and explain how to make it. Use Spelling Words from the list.

Theme 2: **American Stories** 139

Name _____

Identify Parts of a Definition

Choose the correct label for each part of the definition of *family* **from the list. Write the labels in the spaces provided.**

entry word

part of speech

first meaning

second meaning

part of speech

third meaning

fourth meaning

fifth meaning

sixth meaning

sample sentence

syllable break

pronunciation

sample sentence

word form with a

different ending

_____

_____

_____

_____

_____

_____

_____

family *noun* **1.** A group consisting of parents and their children. **2.** The children of a father and a mother; offspring: *We are a large family.* **3.** A group of persons related by blood; relatives. **4.** All the members of a household who live under one roof. **5.** A group of things that share certain features or properties: *English is a member of a larger family of languages.* **6.** A group of related plants or animals.

fam•i•ly (făm′ ə lē) noun, plural, **families**

_____

_____

Name _____

Finding Singular and Plural Nouns

In each sentence, circle each singular common noun.
Underline each plural common noun.

1. Tanya didn't like traveling on buses.

2. In the barnyard, Tanya couldn't see any horses.

3. From inside the house, Tanya saw raindrops on the window.

4. The girl and her cousins played games.

5. Lights far away seemed like torches through the sheets of rain.

6. Patches of ground were soaked.

7. In the kitchen, boxes were scattered all over.

8. The trees in the orchard were full of ripe apples.

Write each plural noun in the correct column below.

Adds _s_ to form the plural	**Adds _es_ to form the plural**
_____	_____
_____	_____
_____	_____
_____	_____
_____	_____
_____	_____
_____	_____

Name _____

Puzzle with Plurals

Complete the crossword puzzle about things that Tanya saw on her trip to the family reunion in Virginia. Use the general clues to write the plural forms of these exact nouns from the story.

ACROSS

3. fields for growing fruit trees
5. rooms for cooking
7. soft, gentle winds
9. daytimes before noon
10. farm buildings

DOWN

1. containers made of cardboard or wood
2. farm birds that lay eggs
4. fees paid to governments
6. body parts for seeing
8. tools for sweeping

Create a Puzzle Use the plural forms of these nouns to create your own crossword on a separate sheet of paper. Trade puzzles with a classmate and complete one another's puzzles.

| porch | horse | pocket |
| glass | bus | farm |

Name _____

Using Exact Nouns

**Read each sentence below. Then rewrite the sentence on the lines below it,
substituting an exact noun for the general noun or words in parentheses.**

1. Everyone was going to a family (get-together).

    _____

    _____

2. Tanya had been on the bus for nine (periods of 60 minutes).

    _____

    _____

3. Tanya grew hungry when she smelled delicious (smells).

    _____

    _____

4. From the porch, Tanya could see the (place where fruit trees grow).

    _____

    _____

5. Before she went to the barn, Tanya put on a pair of (heavy shoes).

    _____

    _____

Name _____

A Character Sketch

Use this page to help you plan a character sketch. Write at least two specific details about what the person looks like, what the person says and does, and how you feel about the person.

Introduction

Whom is my character sketch about?

_____

What the Person Looks Like

Details: 1. _____

2. _____

3. _____

What the Person Says

Details: 1. _____

2. _____

3. _____

What the Person Does

Details: 1. _____

2. _____

3. _____

Conclusion: How I Feel About the Person

_____

_____

On a separate sheet of paper, write your character sketch.

Name _____

Improving Your Writing

► Two or more sentences that run together make a **run-on sentence**.
► Correct run-on sentences by making separate sentences. Add
   sentence end marks and capital letters where they are needed.

**Read the character sketch. Find all the run-on sentences. Then
rewrite the character sketch, including corrections you made.**

My Grandmother

I think my grandmother is my favorite relative, she
knows more than anyone I know. I sometimes wonder if I'll
ever know all that she knows.

She can cook anything you can name, and it always tastes delicious.
You should see her spice cabinet, it's full of all kinds of herbs and spices
for cooking. She says she learned how to use them from her mother and
grandmother.

Sometimes I wonder how she remembers all the things she does.
Maybe I can learn a part of what she knows. Then I'll know a lot about
many things, that's why my grandmother is my favorite relative.

_____

_____

_____

_____

_____

_____

_____

_____

_____

Name _____

Go West!

Like John Stetson, many people traveled west in the 1800s to seek their fortunes. Complete the story by filling in each blank with the correct word from the list. Then answer the question.

Many _____ came from the East to live out West. They were seeking an _____ to make their fortunes. A great number of them were _____ to find gold.

New people were arriving at the _____ almost daily. These people were true _____ who had traveled across the prairie to the Colorado territory. They stayed to become _____ of the new area. Those who drove cattle were called _____. The hide of the cattle was often _____ to make useful items like hats, boots, and belts. In addition, cowboys needed other special _____ for their outdoor work. What piece of equipment might a cowboy need for outdoor work?

_____

Name _____

What's It About?

Complete the description for each part of a three-part documentary about the life of John Stetson.

Television — What's On TV This Week

Monday, 8:00 P.M., Part 1

Twelve-year-old John Batterson Stetson is hard at work in the family's hat-making shop in New Jersey. Young John first hear about the West _____

In 1859, John B. Stetson, now a young man, decides to head west

_____ .

Wednesday, 8:00 P.M., Part 2

John mines for gold and realizes the hat he is wearing offers very little protection from the weather. John decides to make _____

_____ .

One day a horseman rides into camp and _____

_____ .

Thursday, 8:00 P.M., Part 3

John decides to move to Philadelphia and _____

_____ .

The shop is not successful until one day John remembers the horseman who bought his hat. John spends all his money making samples of the hat and sends them _____ .

For weeks, John hears nothing. Then suddenly the orders roll in. In no time, John Stetson's Boss of the Plains _____ .

_____ .

Name _____

General Statements

Read the article below and complete the chart on the following page.

Settling Colorado

Before Colorado became a state in 1876, some Native Americans lived in the mountain valleys and on the plains. A few people wandered through the mountains looking for gold and other valuable minerals. Only a few farming families lived anywhere in the region.

In 1858, people found gold near what is now Denver. Soon, thousands of people had settled in the region. Tiny settlements became large towns. Farmers and ranchers settled in the mountain valleys.

Today, residents of Colorado no longer live in the wide-open spaces of the Old West. Instead, four out of every five people in the region live in one of six large cities. Many people move to these cities every year. Also, many of the mountain areas still have no residents.

Name _____

General Statements continued

In the chart below write the details that answer
the questions. Then form the generalizations.

What was the population like in Colorado before the 1850s?

Details: _____

_____

_____

Generalization: _____

_____

How did Colorado change after the 1850s?

Details: _____

_____

_____

Generalization: _____

_____

What is the population of Colorado like today?

Details: _____

_____

_____

Generalization: _____

_____

Name _____

Super Suffixes

Write the word from the box that matches each clue. Write only one letter on each line. Remember, the endings *-er, -or,* and *-ist* each mean "someone who." If you need help, use a dictionary. To solve the riddle, write the numbered letter from each answer on the line with the matching number.

composer	sailor	teacher
conductor	traveler	settler

1. Someone who sails ___ ___ ___ ___ ___ ___
   ₆

2. Someone who takes a trip ___ ___ ___ ___ ___ ___ ___
   ₁

3. Someone who settles
   a new place ___ ___ ___ ___ ___ ___
   ₅

4. Someone who is in
   charge of a train ___ ___ ___ ___ ___ ___ ___ ___ ___
   ₄

5. Someone who teaches ___ ___ ___ ___ ___ ___ ___
   ₃

6. Someone who writes music ___ ___ ___ ___ ___ ___ ___ ___
   ₂

Riddle: What did the alien say to the book?

Take me to your ___ ___ ___ ___ ___ ___ !
1   2   3   4   5   6

Name _____

The /îr/, /är/, and /âr/ Sounds

When you hear the /îr/, /är/, and /âr/ sounds, think of these patterns and examples:

Patterns	Examples
/îr/ *ear, eer*	g**ear**, ch**eer**
/är/ *ar*	sh**ar**p
/âr/ *are, air*	st**are**, h**air**y

► The spelling patterns for the vowel + *r* sounds in the starred words are different. In *heart*, the /är/ sound is spelled *ear*. In *weird*, the /îr/ sound is spelled *eir*. In *scarce*, the /âr/ sound is spelled *ar*.

Write each Spelling Word under its vowel + *r* sound.

/îr/ Sound

_____   _____

_____   _____

_____   _____

/är/ Sound

_____   _____

_____   _____

_____   _____

/âr/ Sound

_____   _____

_____   _____

_____

Spelling Words

1. gear
2. spear
3. sharp
4. stare
5. alarm
6. cheer
7. square
8. hairy
9. heart*
10. weird*
11. starve
12. charm
13. beard
14. hardly
15. spare
16. stairs
17. year
18. charge
19. dairy
20. scarce*

Spelling Spree

Word Search Write the Spelling Word that is hidden in each sentence.

Example: Ea<u>ch air</u>plane was on time. *chair*

1. Does the diver need air yet? _____

2. This harp has a broken string. _____

3. How often does the spa replace the mud? _____

4. The royal armada sailed the seas. _____

5. Children of that age are cute. _____

6. The show will star very famous people. _____

7. How much armor did knights wear? _____

8. His pea rolled off his fork. _____

Book Titles Write the Spelling Word that best completes each funny book title. **Remember to use capital letters.**

Example: *Something's in the* __Air__
   by Lotta Smoke

9. *Getting by When Money Is* _____ by B. A. Tightwad

10. *Ways to* _____ *Up a Gloomy Pal* by May Kem Laff

11. *Climb the* _____ *to Success* by Rich N. Famous

12. *Taking* _____ *of Your Life* by U. Ken Dewitt

9. _____   11. _____

10. _____   12. _____

Name _____

Proofreading and Writing

Proofreading Circle the five misspelled Spelling Words in this paragraph from a story. Then write each word correctly.

Suddenly, a hush came over the room. I could hardly hear a sound. I turned, and there in the doorway stood a huge cowpoke with a long beerd. I couldn't help but stayre at him because he looked so odd. A Stetson hat sat on his head. His weard hands were as hairy as bear paws. He was covered with dust too. Then he grinned and said shyly, "Howdy, folks!" Someone yelled, "It's Big John, home from a yier on the trail!" The crowd broke into a cheer, and everyone ran up to shake John's hand.

1. gear
2. spear
3. sharp
4. stare
5. alarm
6. cheer
7. square
8. hairy
9. heart*
10. weird*
11. starve
12. charm
13. beard
14. hardly
15. spare
16. stairs
17. year
18. charge
19. dairy
20. scarce*

1. _____   4. _____

2. _____   5. _____

3. _____

✏️— **Write an Ad** If you were to create a new style of hat, what would it look like? Why would people want to buy one of your hats?

On a separate piece of paper, write an ad that tells about your hat. Make the hat seem so great that everyone will want to buy one. Use Spelling Words from the list.

154   Theme 2: **American Stories**

Name _____

It's All in the Context

Choose the correct definition from the list below for each underlined word in the paragraph. Write the letter after the number matching the word. Use context clues to help choose the right definition.

a. to protect or cover
b. small in amount
c. explore for valuable metals
d. one-of-a-kind
e. the flat, broad lower edge of a hat

f. beautiful; scenic
g. setting a person or thing apart from others
h. a rock containing gold or silver
i. strike out; make a new path
j. a remote area with few people

John Stetson and the Pikes Peakers headed away from the cities and into the frontier.
₁ Along the way, they passed picturesque
₂ landscapes that seemed to be painted in red and gold. John's distinctive
₃ hat made him stand out from the rest. It was unique
₄; no one else had anything like it. John liked the way the hat's wide brim
₅ managed to shield
₆ his face from the sun. When they reached Colorado, John saw men prospect
₇ for gold. In some rocks they found ore
₈ containing silver. Mostly, though, results were so meager
₉ that many miners left Colorado to blaze
₁₀ a new trail to the California goldfields.

1. _____
2. _____
3. _____
4. _____
5. _____
6. _____
7. _____
8. _____
9. _____
10. _____

Name _____

Finding More Plural Nouns

Underline each plural noun in the sentences below.

1. The West offered many opportunities for making money.

2. In Eastern cities, a Stetson hat wouldn't sell.

3. In the territories of the West, many men wore one.

4. Behind many a herd of sheep rode a cowboy with a Stetson.

5. A horse might carry a settler's supplies, but the settler wore his
   Stetson.

6. Ladies were impressed by a stylish broad-brimmed hat.

7. If you picked berries, you could always put them in your Stetson.

8. Did anyone ever see sheep or deer wearing headgear like that?

**On the line at the right of each singular noun given, write the
correct plural form. Use a dictionary to help you.**

9. duty _____

10. woman _____

11. bison _____

12. sky _____

13. moose _____

14. child _____

15. ditty _____

.

Rewriting Plural Nouns

Rewrite each sentence on the lines provided, using the plural of the noun in parentheses.

1. Many (family) went west to seek wealth.

   _____

2. Some came from (city) in the East.

   _____

3. Hats like (derby) were not useful in bad weather.

   _____

4. In this new land, people needed special kinds of (supply).

   _____

5. (Man) who worked in the open needed a hat to protect them.

   _____

6. Against (sky) full of rain or snow, a Stetson offered protection.

   _____

7. Herders of (sheep) wanted to keep the sun out of their eyes.

   _____

8. John Stetson's new hat pleased cowboys and (woman) alike.

   _____

9. In all the (territory) you could see Stetsons everywhere.

   _____

10. Everyone, including (child), sported a Stetson.

   _____

Name _____

Proofreading for Noun Endings

Proofread the paragraph below. Find plurals of nouns that are incorrectly spelled. Circle each misspelled plural. Then correctly write each misspelled plural on the lines provided. Use a dictionary to help you.

Proofreading Marks ⬭ spell correctly

Would you like a hat to protect you from rainy skyes? How about one to keep the sun out of your eyies? You can use these hats to hold grainies for your horsers or to carry freshly picked strawberris. You can make two earholes in these hats and put them on your sheeps or oxes. What kind of hat can entire familys wear — men, woman, and childs? Are they derbys? No, these hats are Stetsones.

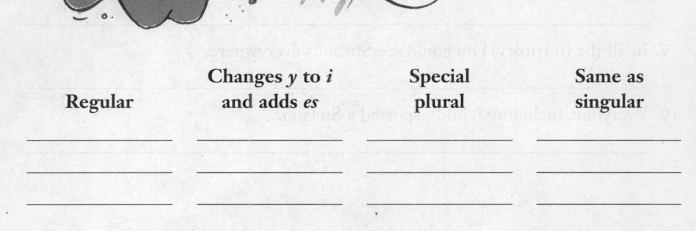

Regular	Changes *y* to *i* and adds *es*	Special plural	Same as singular
_____	_____	_____	_____
_____	_____	_____	_____
_____	_____	_____	_____
_____	_____	_____	_____

Name _____

Writing a Business Letter

Use this page to help you plan a business letter.

My Purpose for Writing _____

Writer's Address   _____

_____

_____   Inside Address

_____

_____

_____   Greeting

Introductory Paragraph

_____

_____

_____

Middle Paragraph

_____

_____

_____

Concluding Paragraph

_____

_____

_____

Closing

_____

Signature

_____

Improving Your Writing

Read the business letter. Find details that do not keep to the point. Mark them to be deleted. Then recopy the letter, with these details omitted, on another sheet of paper.

1407 Green Street
Urbana, Illinois 61801
January 19, 2001

Ms. Angela O'Byrne
Public Relations Director
Kitchenwares Incorporated
920 Main Street
Mineola, New York 11502

Dear Ms. O'Byrne:

I am writing to request information about the new Whiz food processor. I am in the cooking class at school. We are learning to bake now. Our class needs a new processor. We saw an advertisement in the newspaper. The processor in your ad seems to be a good one.

Our teacher asked me to write to you for information about what the processor costs and what it will do. I like to write. I always get good grades on my compositions. I will take the information you send and present it to our class. The class will decide if the Whiz is the one for us.

Thank you for your help. I hope the Whiz will be the food processor that we get for our class. I am sure the information you send will help us make our decision.

Sincerely,
Maria Lopez

Name _____

Becoming a Citizen

Miguel's grandparents want to become citizens, but they don't know what to do. Miguel tells them what to expect. Complete Miguel's story by filling in each blank with the correct word from the list.

Vocabulary

allegiance
chamber
citizen
citizenship
enrich
examiner
oath
petitioners

When someone wants to become a _____ of the United States, that person must go through a special ceremony. The ceremony takes place in a United States government courthouse. The people all gather in a room called a _____. When everyone is seated, a person called an _____ calls out each person's name. Then each of the _____ walks up to the desk, is given a certificate, and signs his or her name. After this is done, a judge comes into the room to administer the _____ of _____. All the people stand up and pledge their _____ to the United States. After the ceremony, friends and relatives offer their congratulations to the new citizens. Hopefully, the new citizens will _____ their lives and the lives of others as citizens of their new country.

Name _____

Who/What Chart

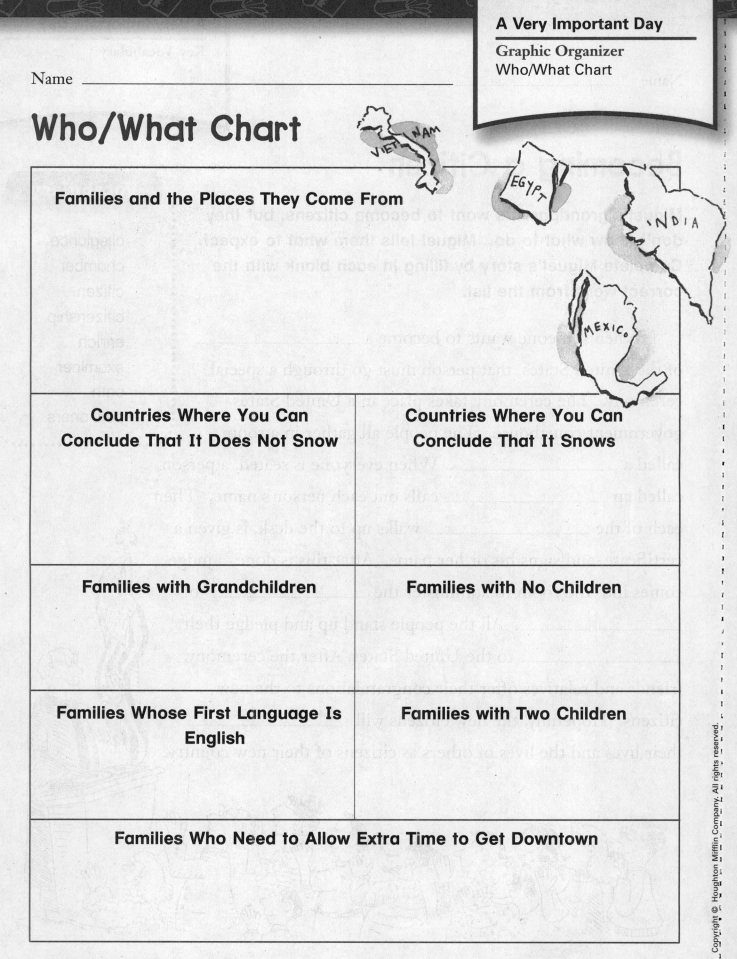

Families and the Places They Come From	
Countries Where You Can Conclude That It Does Not Snow	**Countries Where You Can Conclude That It Snows**
Families with Grandchildren	**Families with No Children**
Families Whose First Language Is English	**Families with Two Children**
Families Who Need to Allow Extra Time to Get Downtown	

Name _____

The /ôr/, /ûr/, and /yo͝or/ Sounds

When you hear the /ôr/, /ûr/, or /yo͝or/ sounds, think of these patterns and examples:

Patterns	Examples
/ôr/ *or, ore*	h**or**se, ch**ore**
/ûr/ *ur, ir, ear, or*	f**ir**m, c**ur**ve, l**ear**n, w**or**m
/yo͝or/ *ure*	p**ure**

► The /ôr/ sound is usually spelled *or* or *ore*.
► They /ûr/ sound is usually spelled *ir, ur, ear,* or *or*.
► The /yo͝or/ sound is usually spelled *ure*.
► The spelling patterns for the /ôr/ sounds in the starred words *board* and *course* are different.

Write each Spelling Word under its vowel + *r* sounds.

/ôr/ Sounds

_____   _____
_____   _____
_____   _____

/ûr/ Sounds

_____   _____
_____   _____
_____   _____
_____   _____
_____   _____

/yo͝or/ Sounds

_____   _____

Name _____

Spelling Spree

Word Addition Write a Spelling Word by adding the beginning of the first word to the end of the second word.

Example: hum + part *hurt*

1. curb + dive _____
2. chop + store _____
3. wool + corn _____
4. seat + march _____
5. cut + girl _____
6. fix + term _____
7. boat + hard _____
8. cut + tore _____
9. ship + dart _____
10. put + care _____

Questions Write a Spelling Word to answer each question.

11. What number is one more than twelve?
12. What is the name for a large animal that has a long mane?
13. What word describes a room that has not been cleaned?
14. What small, soft-bodied animal crawls through the soil?
15. What do you do when you hit a home run in baseball?

11. _____   14. _____
12. _____   15. _____
13. _____

168   Theme 2: **American Stories**

Spelling Words

1. horse
2. chore
3. firm
4. learn
5. dirty
6. curve
7. world
8. pure
9. board*
10. course*
11. heard
12. return
13. cure
14. score
15. worm
16. thirteen
17. worn
18. curl
19. shirt
20. search

Name _____

Proofreading and Writing

Proofreading Circle the five misspelled Spelling Words
in this friendly letter. Then write each word correctly.

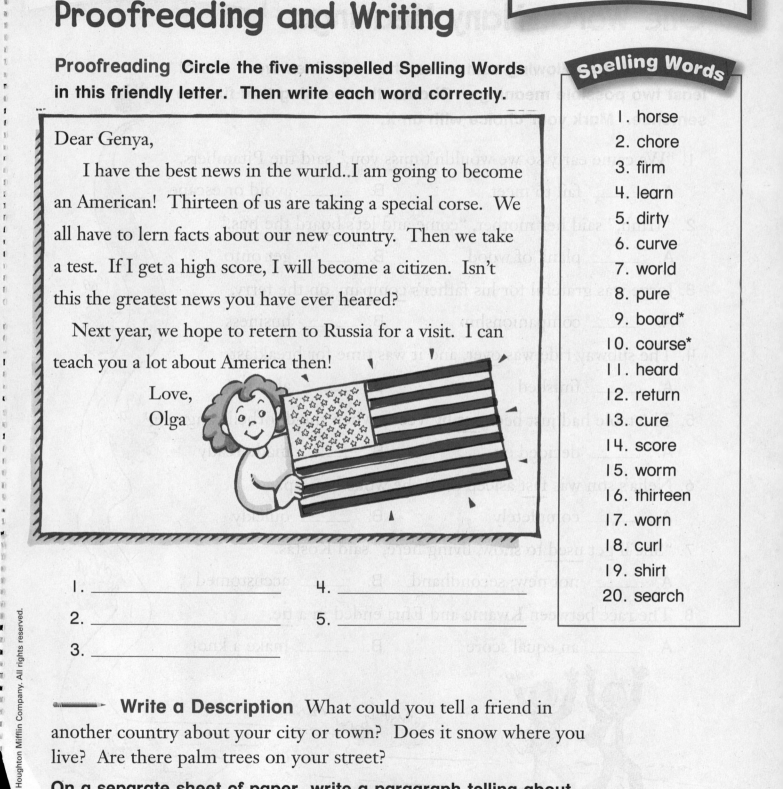

Dear Genya,

    I have the best news in the wurld..I am going to become
an American! Thirteen of us are taking a special corse. We
all have to lern facts about our new country. Then we take
a test. If I get a high score, I will become a citizen. Isn't
this the greatest news you have ever heared?

    Next year, we hope to retern to Russia for a visit. I can
teach you a lot about America then!

Love,
Olga

Spelling Words

1. horse
2. chore
3. firm
4. learn
5. dirty
6. curve
7. world
8. pure
9. board*
10. course*
11. heard
12. return
13. cure
14. score
15. worm
16. thirteen
17. worn
18. curl
19. shirt
20. search

1. _____ 4. _____

2. _____ 5. _____

3. _____

✏️➤ **Write a Description** What could you tell a friend in
another country about your city or town? Does it snow where you
live? Are there palm trees on your street?

**On a separate sheet of paper, write a paragraph telling about
the place where you live. Use Spelling Words from the list.**

Name _____

One Word, Many Meanings

In each of the following sentences, the underlined word has at least two possible meanings. Choose the meaning that fits the sentence. Mark your choice with an X.

1. "We came early so we wouldn't <u>miss</u> you," said the Pitambers.

   A. _____ fail to meet   B. _____ avoid or escape

2. "Trinh," said her mother, "come and let's <u>board</u> the bus."

   A. _____ plank of wood   B. _____ get onto

3. Jorge was grateful for his father's <u>company</u> on the ferry.

   A. _____ companionship   B. _____ business

4. The subway ride was <u>over</u>, and it was time for breakfast.

   A. _____ finished   B. _____ above

5. The table had just been <u>set</u> by Veena when the doorbell rang.

   A. _____ decided on   B. _____ made ready

6. Nelia's son was <u>fast</u> asleep until she woke him up.

   A. _____ completely   B. _____ quickly

7. "She'll get <u>used</u> to snow, living here," said Kostas.

   A. _____ not new; secondhand   B. _____ accustomed

8. The race between Kwame and Efua ended in a <u>tie</u>.

   A. _____ an equal score   B. _____ make a knot

Name _____

In Search of Possessive Nouns

In each sentence, underline each possessive noun form.

1. Nelia's family in the Philippines had never seen snow.

2. Miguel's family was going to the courthouse.

3. The Patels' neighbors and children were invited to breakfast.

4. Eugenia's whole family took the subway downtown.

5. Grandfather's hands were full of wet snow.

6. Mrs. Soutsos laughed at little Kiki's reaction to snowflakes.

7. The family's restaurant was closed for the day.

8. Passengers' bundles fell to the floor when the driver had to stop.

9. The judge's voice was loud and clear in the courtroom.

10. The citizens' voices could be heard saying the Pledge of Allegiance.

On the line at the right of each noun, write the correct possessive form.

11. relative _____   16. sister _____

12. woman _____   17. mouse _____

13. children _____   18. babies _____

14. Eugenia _____   19. crowd _____

15. friends _____   20. city _____

Name _____

Replacing with Possessive Nouns

Rewrite each sentence, replacing the underlined words with a singular or plural possessive noun.

1. Nelia heard <u>the voice of the announcer</u> telling about the snow.

   _____

2. <u>The sister of Miguel</u> woke him up.

   _____

3. Niko, <u>the brother of Kiko</u>, helped her sweep snow off
   the sidewalk.

   _____

4. Everyone in <u>the family of the Leonovs</u> had waited for the big day.

   _____

5. Down from the window came a gift from <u>a friend of Yujin</u>.

   _____

6. Becoming a citizen was <u>the goal of an immigrant</u>.

   _____

7. Everyone heard the examiner call out each of <u>the names of
   the Castros</u>.

   _____

8. All the people in the room could hear <u>the words of the judge</u>.

   _____

Name _____

Proofreading for Apostrophes

**Proofread each sentence. Find any possessive
nouns that lack apostrophes or have apostrophes in
the wrong place. Circle each incorrect possessive
noun. Then write the corrected sentence on the line
below it.**

1. The days main event for many families was becoming
United States citizens.

_____

_____

2. To one womans surprise, the DJ predicted six inches of snow.

_____

_____

3. The Huerta familys goal was to be at the courthouse early.

_____

_____

4. Kwames wife, Efua, had her picture taken.

_____

_____

5. All the Castros signatures were on the court papers.

_____

_____

Name _____

Writing Journal Entries

Answer these questions. Then use your answers to help write your own journal entry.

1. What new word, fact, or idea did you learn today? Now, write it down, along with a few words telling why you found it interesting.

   _____

   _____

2. If you could ask anybody in the world a question, who would that person be and what question would you ask?

   _____

   _____

3. As you look around, what object catches your eye? Name the object, and write a few words to describe it.

   _____

   _____

4. What is a recent movie or television show that you've seen? Now, give your opinion of it.

   _____

   _____

5. What is one thing that makes you smile? Write what it is and why it makes you smile.

   _____

   _____

Name _____

Improving Your Writing

Suppose Kostas kept a journal. Read the journal entry below. Then write a journal entry as if you were one of the other characters in *A Very Important Day*. Write your observations and feelings in words that give your writing your own personal voice.

From Kostas's Journal

January 18

Today will be very special. Mother and Father are becoming United States citizens. I don't have to do that, because I'm already a citizen. I was born in this country. I feel very proud that they will become citizens, too. Tonight, we'll have a wonderful party to celebrate.

It is snowing. I like snow. The city becomes quieter when it snows. The street sounds are muffled, and the city seems peaceful. I hope there will be enough snow to make a snowman. Maybe there will be enough snow to make two!

_____

_____

_____

_____

_____

_____

_____

_____

_____

Name _____

Come Fly with Us!

Complete the sentences in this advertisement. Use each vocabulary word only once.

Learn to Fly Today!

Have you ever thought about learning how to fly? At the Right Flight School, we can help you get your pilot's _____. Our classroom lectures teach you about the instruments found in the _____ and how to use them when you fly. We'll show you how to fly high over the clouds and at lower _____ too.

Are you looking to pilot a plane by yourself? We'll have you flying _____ before you know it! And for your convenience, you'll get to take off and land from our own private _____.

Come by to see if the Right Flight School is right for you!

Name _____

Inferring Characters

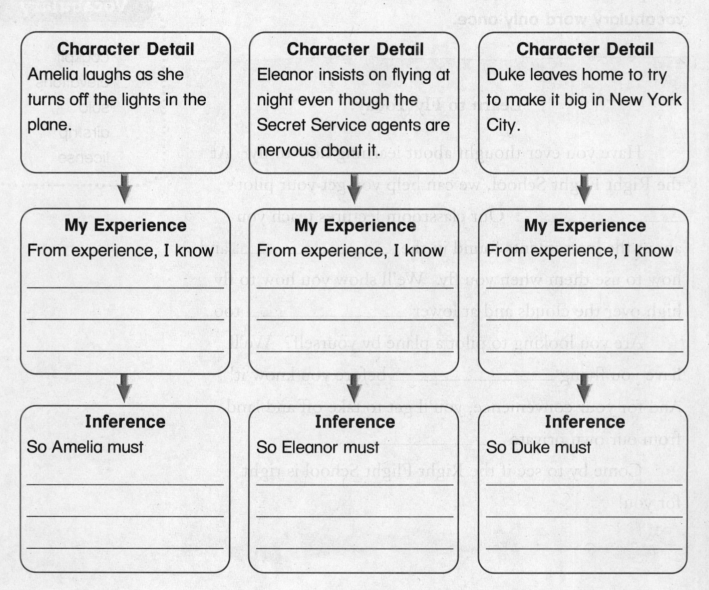

Character Detail
Amelia laughs as she turns off the lights in the plane.

Character Detail
Eleanor insists on flying at night even though the Secret Service agents are nervous about it.

Character Detail
Duke leaves home to try to make it big in New York City.

My Experience
From experience, I know
_____
_____
_____

My Experience
From experience, I know
_____
_____
_____

My Experience
From experience, I know
_____
_____
_____

Inference
So Amelia must
_____
_____
_____

Inference
So Eleanor must
_____
_____
_____

Inference
So Duke must
_____
_____
_____

Name _____

Compare and Contrast Inferences

The author of *Amelia and Eleanor Go for a Ride* shows Amelia Earhart and Eleanor Roosevelt in action. You can use what the author shows to make inferences about what the two women are like. Think of words to describe each woman's traits. Think of words to describe the traits of two other people you have read about in this theme. Write your ideas in the chart.

Name of Person or Character	What He or She Is Like	Why I Think So
Amelia Earhart		
Eleanor Roosevelt		

Name _____

Jazz Words

Choose the best meaning for the underlined word. Write the letter of your answer on the line provided.

1. The <u>orchestra</u> practiced their music all week for the Friday concert. _____
   A. band leader   B. group of friends   C. dancers   D. group of musicians

2. I forgot the rest of the piece I was playing, so I decided to <u>improvise</u> some
   new music. _____
   A. make up   B. stop playing   C. forget   D. sing

3. He is a great pianist and loves to play <u>ragtime</u> tunes. _____
   A. dishtowel   B. classical   C. a type of jazz   D. very easy

4. This new radio station plays <u>melodies</u> I have never heard before. _____
   A. songs or tunes   B. video games   C. ads   D. reporters

5. Clara says that when it is raining outside, she sometimes gets the <u>blues</u>. _____
   A. sky colors   B. sad feelings   C. hungry   D. wet

6. Eduardo wrote an essay celebrating his Mexican <u>heritage</u>. _____
   A. new home   B. vacation   C. cultural traditions   D. country

7. Those two trumpet players are members of a famous <u>jazz</u> band. _____
   A. a type of music   B. rubber string   C. musician   D. professional

Now take three of the vocabulary words above and use them all in one sentence.

_____

_____

Test Practice

Use the three steps you've learned to complete these sentences about *Duke Ellington*. Fill in the circle for the best answer in the answer rows at the bottom of each page.

1. As a boy, Duke did not like his piano lessons because _____.

   A the music was too difficult

   B he did not like his piano teacher

   C he wanted to learn to play the trumpet instead

   D the music he had to play was boring

2. Duke changed his mind about the piano the first time he heard _____.

   F a record owned by Joe Nanton

   G ragtime music

   H a choir in Harlem

   J Greer's drum playing

3. Duke and his band first played in _____.

   A Washington, D. C.   **C** Harlem

   B Kalamazoo   **D** Hollywood

4. **Connecting/Comparing** John Stetson from *Boss of the Plains* is similar to Duke Ellington because _____.

   F they both got discouraged and gave up their dreams

   G they both created something that became very popular

   H they both learned the family business

   J they both played at the most famous jazz club in New York City

ANSWER ROWS	1 Ⓐ Ⓑ Ⓒ Ⓓ	3 Ⓐ Ⓑ Ⓒ Ⓓ
	2 Ⓕ Ⓖ Ⓗ Ⓙ	4 Ⓕ Ⓖ Ⓗ Ⓙ

Continue on page 182.

Theme 2: **American Stories**   181

Test Practice continued

5. On page 276N, the author writes that *Duke painted colors with his band's sound* to show that Duke's music _____.

   A was often sad

   B blended the sounds of all the musicians in his band

   C made people think of paintings in a museum

   D had a strong beat

6. Duke took his band to New York because _____.

   F he wanted to sell a record that his band had made

   G the people in Washington, D. C. did not like the band's music

   H the people in New York had never heard ragtime music

   J he wanted the band to play in Harlem

7. After Duke's band first played at the Cotton Club, _____.

   A Duke heard ragtime music for the first time

   B Duke decided to call his band the Washingtonians

   C Duke's band grew larger and changed its name

   D Duke's band moved away from New York City

8. **Connecting/Comparing** Grandma from *Tanya's Reunion* might like Duke's song *Black, Brown, and Beige* because _____.

   F the song honors African American history

   G Grandma often talks about ragtime music

   H Duke Ellington grew up on a farm in Virginia

   J the song tells the story of a family reunion

ANSWER ROWS	5 Ⓐ Ⓑ Ⓒ Ⓓ	7 Ⓐ Ⓑ Ⓒ Ⓓ
	6 Ⓕ Ⓖ Ⓗ Ⓙ	8 Ⓕ Ⓖ Ⓗ Ⓙ

Name _____

What Happened When?

Complete the Event Map below by filling in important
events from *Duke Ellington.*

Page 276H

As a child Duke quit his piano lessons, but later he

_____

_____

Page 276I

When Duke was nineteen,

_____

_____

Page 276J

In 1927

_____

_____ .

Page 276N

In 1939

_____

_____ .

Page 276P

In January 1943

_____

_____ .

Generally Speaking

Read the paragraph below.

> When Amelia Earhart suggested that she and Eleanor Roosevelt take a night flight together, the Secret Service men protested. After all, their job is to keep the President and his family safe. Public officials and their families are always at risk when they travel. As a result, wherever they go, members of the President's family are usually accompanied by Secret Service agents. The idea of the First Lady flying alone with a friend at night would alarm any Secret Service agent.

Find three statements in the paragraph that are generalizations. Write the generalizations below.

1. _____
   _____

2. _____
   _____

3. _____
   _____

Think about the night flight Amelia and Eleanor took. Write two general statements about what night flights are like.

4. _____
   _____

5. _____
   _____

Name _____

Put Possessives in Place

Possessive	**Meaning**
<u>plane's</u> wings	wings of the plane
<u>friends'</u> scarves	scarves of/belonging to the friends
<u>people's</u> curiosity	curiosity of the people
<u>Roosevelts'</u> home	home of/belonging to the Roosevelts

Read each sentence below. Rewrite each underlined phrase, using a possessive noun.

1. Eleanor accepted the <u>offer of Amelia</u> to fly at night.

   _____

2. She ignored the <u>protests of the Secret Service men.</u>

   _____

3. Amelia led the plane down the <u>runway of the airport.</u>

   _____

4. Soon, the <u>laughter of the friends</u> filled the night sky.

   _____

5. Amelia turned off all of the <u>lights of the plane.</u>

   _____

6. The <u>dome of the Capitol</u> glowed in the moonlight.

   _____

7. Afterwards, the women answered the <u>questions of reporters.</u>

   _____

8. Then they 'flew' off in the <u>car of the First Lady.</u>

   _____

Which Meaning Is Correct?

Read the definitions. Then read each sentence below the definitions. Choose the correct meaning for the underlined word. Write the number of the meaning in the blank.

> **band** (bănd) *noun* **1.** A group of animals or people. **2.** Musicians who play together.
>
> **club** (klŭb) *noun* **1.** A heavy stick. **2.** A place used for a certain purpose.
>
> **com•pa•ny** (kŭm′ pə nē) *noun* **1.** A gathering of people. **2.** A guest or guests. **3.** A companion or companions. **4.** A business.
>
> **out•fit** (out′ fĭt′) *noun* **1.** A set of equipment for a particular purpose. **2.** A set of clothing that goes together.
>
> **step** (stĕp) *noun* **1.** A movement made by picking up one foot and putting it down. **2.** Distance covered by such a movement. **3.** The sound of someone walking. **4.** One of a set of stairs. **5.** Any of the stages in a process. **6.** A fixed movement, as in dancing.

1. Men and women in stylish <u>outfits</u> lined up outside the Plantation in New York City. _____

2. The lively <u>company</u> of fans laughed and joked as they waited for the doors to open. _____

3. The great Duke Ellington was appearing with his orchestra at the <u>club</u> that night. _____

4. News of the <u>band</u> and its exciting music had spread throughout the nation. _____

5. Soon the music lovers would be inside the club, out on the dance floor, trying out the latest <u>steps</u>. _____

Name _____

Spelling Review

Write Spelling Words from the list on this page to answer the questions.

1–14. Which fourteen words have the /ou/, /ô/, /ŏŏ/, or /ōō/ sounds?

1. _____ 8. _____
2. _____ 9. _____
3. _____ 10. _____
4. _____ 11. _____
5. _____ 12. _____
6. _____ 13. _____
7. _____ 14. _____

15–22. Which eight words have the /îr/, /är/, or /âr/ sounds?

15. _____ 19. _____
16. _____ 20. _____
17. _____ 21. _____
18. _____ 22. _____

23–30. Which eight words have the /ôr/ or /ûr/ sounds?

23. _____ 27. _____
24. _____ 28. _____
25. _____ 29. _____
26. _____ 30. _____

Spelling Words

1. gear
2. howl
3. wood
4. bounce
5. jaw
6. put
7. year
8. false
9. couch
10. dawn
11. push
12. sauce
13. spare
14. tool
15. full
16. search
17. roof
18. pull
19. hardly
20. world
21. dairy
22. chore
23. curl
24. dirty
25. alarm
26. cheer
27. charge
28. horse
29. heard
30. return

Name _____

Spelling Spree

Context Clues Write the Spelling Word that completes each sentence.

1. You rode a black _____ at the farm.

2. When I come back, I _____.

3. I _____ my coat in the closet.

4. We _____ noises in the kitchen.

5. Mom likes to _____ her hair.

Rhyme Time Write the Spelling Word that makes sense and rhymes with the word in dark print.

6. **Thirty** _____ rabbits hopped.

7. We always **yawn** at _____.

8. **Ouch**! I fell off of the _____.

9. Choose **good** _____ for the fire.

10. Wolves sometimes **growl** or _____.

American Places Use the Spelling Words to complete these sentences about American cities.

11. New York is one of the biggest cities in the _____.

12. There are many _____ farms in Wisconsin.

13. Many people visit Austin, Texas, each _____.

14. Sometimes you can _____ see in the fog of San Francisco.

15. Boston chefs make delicious spaghetti _____.

Spelling Words

1. howl
2. couch
3. dawn
4. sauce
5. wood
6. put
7. hardly
8. year
9. dairy
10. horse
11. dirty
12. curl
13. heard
14. world
15. return

Name _____

Proofreading and Writing

Proofreading Circle the six misspelled Spelling Words in this advertisement. Then write each word correctly.

Come visit a real log cabin. You will bownce along an old lane for about one mile. Then you will see smoke from the chimney on the ruf. The charg is three dollars.

In the 1700s, people had little spair time. Each child had at least one chor to do. Every day was ful of work.

1. _____	4. _____
2. _____	5. _____
3. _____	6. _____

Spelling Words

1. alarm
2. false
3. tool
4. jaw
5. charge
6. full
7. roof
8. chore
9. search
10. pull
11. gear
12. spare
13. bounce
14. cheer
15. push

What's the Message? After his visit, Harry e-mailed his cousin. Use Spelling Words to complete the message.

Is it true or 7. _____ that you are sick? I hope this note will 8. _____ you up. My 9. _____ dropped when we visited a log cabin. No 10. _____ in the cabin was electric! You would need muscles to 11. _____ and 12. _____ logs into place! Except for a fire 13. _____ in the roof, it is the same as it was long ago. We can 14. _____ for a place like this where we can bring our camping 15. _____.

✏️ **Write a Diary Entry** On a separate sheet of paper, write a diary entry about life in a log cabin. Use the Spelling Review Words.

Name _____

Identifying Proper Nouns

Underline the proper nouns in each sentence. Then write each proper noun in the correct space below.

1. Amelia Earhart flew an airplane called the Curtis Condor.

2. She and Eleanor Roosevelt flew the loop from Washington, D.C. to Baltimore and back.

3. No one from the Secret Service accompanied them.

4. They flew over the Potomac River.

5. Reporters from the Washington Post interviewed the women after their flight.

6. Later, the two friends returned to the White House.

Write each underlined proper noun in the correct space below.

Person	Place	Thing
_____	_____	_____
_____	_____	_____
_____	_____	_____

Name _____

Identifying Singular and Plural Nouns

In each sentence, circle each singular common noun. Underline each plural common noun. Then write each plural noun in the correct column below.

1. The pilot described her experiences to her friend.
2. Flights at night offer amazing sights.
3. Stars glitter in the dark sky.
4. Clouds shine with a white light.
5. Patches of darkness are parts of the sea.
6. Red flashes mark the tops of towers.

Add -s to form the plural.	**Add -es to form the plural.**
_____	_____
_____	_____
_____	
_____	
_____	
_____	

Name _____

A Puzzle About Plays

Complete the crossword puzzle using words from the vocabulary box.

Vocabulary

act	perform
actor	scene
character	setting
dialogue	stage
lines	theater

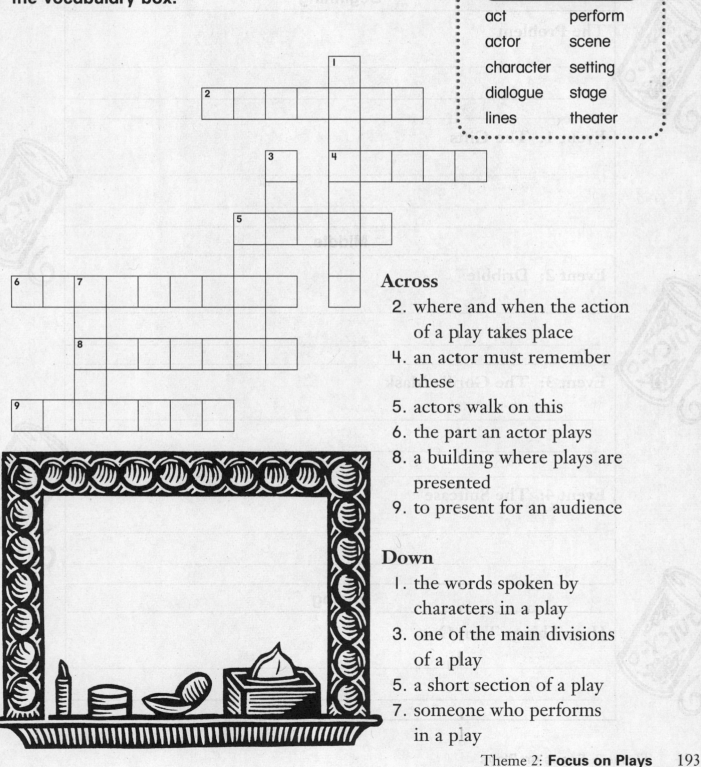

Across

2. where and when the action of a play takes place
4. an actor must remember these
5. actors walk on this
6. the part an actor plays
8. a building where plays are presented
9. to present for an audience

Down

1. the words spoken by characters in a play
3. one of the main divisions of a play
5. a short section of a play
7. someone who performs in a play

Name _____

Plot Map

Beginning

The Problem

_____

_____

Event 1: The Gifts

_____

_____

_____

Middle

Event 2: Dribble

_____

_____

Event 3: The Gorilla Mask

_____

_____

Event 4: The Suitcase

_____

_____

Ending

How Things Turn Out

_____

_____

_____

Name _____

Write a Character Analysis

Write a character analysis, or description, for the following characters from *Tales of a Fourth Grade Nothing*. Describe what kind of person the character is. Be sure to use descriptive adjectives that tell about the character's personality. Refer to the play for examples to support your descriptions.

1. Peter: _____

_____

_____

_____

_____

_____

_____

_____

_____

2. Mrs. Yarby: _____

_____

_____

_____

_____

_____

_____

_____

_____

Name _____

Adapting a Book to a Play

Choose a book (or one of the selections from the previous themes) to adapt into a play. Explain why you have chosen it. Make a list of all the elements of a play that must be included.

_____

_____

_____

_____

_____

_____

Next write the cast of characters, the setting, and the time of the play.

_____

_____

_____

_____

_____

_____

_____

_____

_____

_____

_____

Name _____

Character Development

Review each event in the play *Tales of a Fourth Grade Nothing.*
Write how the Hatcher family members behave in each event.
Then follow the directions below.

Event 1: The Gifts
_____
_____

Event 2: Dribble
_____
_____

Event 3: The Gorilla Mask
_____
_____

Event 4: The Suitcase
_____
_____

How Things Turn Out
_____

Describe the Hatcher family. Use two examples of their actions
to support your description.

_____

_____

_____

_____

Name _____

An Actor's Answers

The word endings *-er*, *-or*, and *-ist* may be suffixes that mean
"someone who."

   A *player* is someone who *plays*.

   An *actor* is someone who *acts*.

   An *artist* is someone who makes *art*.

In some words, *er*, *or*, and *ist* are not suffixes.
They are part of the word.

   number   humor   insist

**Read this interview. Circle words with the suffix *-er*, *-or*, or *-ist*
meaning "someone who." Then write the words on the chart.**

Q: Why do you like being an actor?

A: Acting lets me be many different people. I can be a scientist or a
     sailor. I can be a banker or a bicyclist. I'm eager for new roles.

Q: Did you like playing a famous Olympic swimmer in your last play?

A: Yes! The writer helped me bring that role to life.

Q: Does any other worker help you?

A: The costume designer helps me pick clothes of the right color.
     The director guides my every move. My little sister always tells me
     if I made an error!

-er words	**-or words**	**-ist words**
1._____	6._____	9._____
2._____	7._____	10._____
3._____	8._____	
4._____		
5._____		

Name _____

More Homophones

Homophones are words that sound alike but have different meanings and spellings. When you write a homophone, be sure to spell the word that has the meaning you want.

Write each Spelling Word under the heading that names its vowel sound.

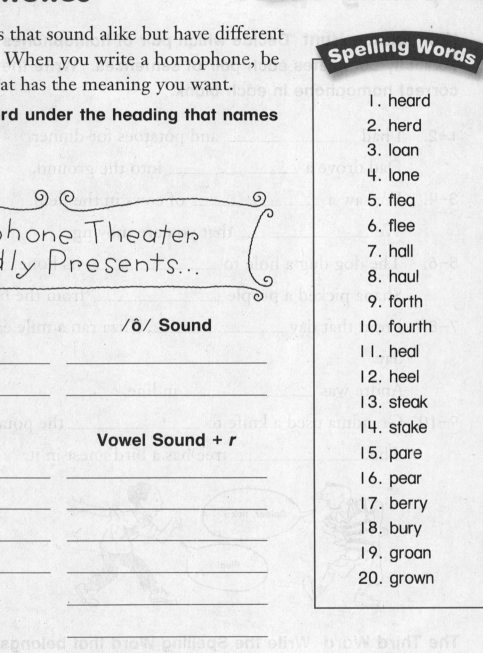

Homophone Theater
Proudly Presents...

/ā/ Sound

_____

_____

/ē/ Sound

_____

_____

_____

/ô/ Sound

_____

_____

Vowel Sound + *r*

_____

_____

_____

/ō/ Sound

_____

_____

_____

1. heard
2. herd
3. loan
4. lone
5. flea
6. flee
7. hall
8. haul
9. forth
10. fourth
11. heal
12. heel
13. steak
14. stake
15. pare
16. pear
17. berry
18. bury
19. groan
20. grown

Name _____

Spelling Spree

Homophone Hunt Decide which pair of homophones correctly completes each pair of sentences. Write the correct homophone in each blank.

1-2. I had _____ and potatoes for dinner.

Dad drove a _____ into the ground.

3-4. We saw a _____ of cows in the field.

We _____ that you are moving.

5-6. The dog dug a hole to _____ its bone.

Shana picked a purple _____ from the bush.

7-8. From that day _____, Eliza ran a mile each day.

Andre was _____ in line.

9-10. Grandma used a knife to _____ the potatoes.

The _____ tree has a bird's nest in it.

Spelling Words

1. heard
2. herd
3. loan
4. lone
5. flea
6. flee
7. hall
8. haul
9. forth
10. fourth
11. heal
12. heel
13. steak
14. stake
15. pare
16. pear
17. berry
18. bury
19. groan
20. grown

Spider, tick . . .

Flea!

The Third Word Write the Spelling Word that belongs in each group.

11. cure, fix, _____

12. one, only, _____

13. carry, pull, _____

14. sigh, grunt, _____

15. run, escape, _____

16. toe, ankle, _____

Name _____

Proofreading and Writing

Proofreading Circle the five incorrect Spelling Words in this short scene from a play. Then write the correct homophones.

Scene: A bank. A banker is working behind a desk. A man walks in. In the haul outside of the bank door stands a furry dog that is the size of an elephant.

MAN: Hi. Will you please lone me some money?

BANKER: Sure. Fill out this form.

MAN: Oh. I herd that you would just give me the money.

BANKER: Well, what do you need the money for?

MAN: My dog needs a new flee collar. He's groan so much!

BANKER: We don't give money for small purchases.

MAN: Well, he isn't a small dog.

1. heard
2. herd
3. loan
4. lone
5. flea
6. flee
7. hall
8. haul
9. forth
10. fourth
11. heal
12. heel
13. steak
14. stake
15. pare
16. pear
17. berry
18. bury
19. groan
20. grown

1. _____   3. _____   5. _____

2. _____   4. _____

✏️ **Make a Poster** Think of an idea for a play. On a separate paper, draw a poster that shows something about the play. Then write headlines and a few sentences to describe it. Use Spelling Words from the list.

Name _____

Clip It

Fill in each blank with a clipped word made from the underlined word.

While eating her <u>luncheon</u> _____, Natalie glanced

at her <u>memorandum</u> _____ pad. "It's time to <u>telephone</u>

_____ the <u>veterinarian</u> _____," she said to

herself.

"Have you finished Fido's <u>examination</u> _____?"
Natalie asked the doctor.

"Yes," said the doctor. "Fido was checked by a team of

<u>professionals</u> _____, and the <u>laboratory</u> _____

tests show that he has no broken bones. You can come pick him up."

Quickly, Natalie put away the remains of her <u>hamburger</u>

_____. She called for a <u>taxicab</u> _____.

"Fido deserves a treat after the ordeal he has been through,"
Natalie told herself. "But, really, he should have known better.
What made him think he could ride a <u>bicycle</u> _____?"

Name _____

Details at Play

Underline the added details in each sentence. Then write on the line the noun that the details describe.

Example: Our school, <u>Bridgeview Elementary School</u>, puts on a play each spring. <u>school</u>

1. Our school play, *Tales of a Fourth Grade Nothing*, was a big hit._____

2. I played the part of Fudge, Peter's little brother.

   _____

3. We used a hand puppet to play the part of Dribble, a lovable turtle. _____

4. Two best friends, Jordan and Marika, played the parts of Mom and Dad. _____

5. Alana Spano, a really funny actor, got lots of laughs playing Mrs. Yarby. _____

6. Our school principal, Mr. Juarez, came to watch the performance. _____

7. I think our biggest fan was Ms. Walton, the gym teacher.

   _____

8. A local newspaper, *The Daily Ledger*, printed a photograph of the whole cast. _____

Name _____

Different Details

You're the director. Choose different details from the box to complete this play description. Be sure that each detail you choose makes sense in the blank. Place a comma before and after each added detail.

Details

a young student

a poodle puppy

a lizard from Mars

a popular movie star

a Spanish teacher

an ice skater

a silly clown

a baby turtle

an excellent juggler

a giant robot

The play's main character _____ begins with a long speech. Then the character's best friend _____ comes along. They meet their neighbor _____ and plan a picnic.

All of a sudden, the stage lights dim. The play's villain _____ arrives, wearing a long black cape. The friends don't know what to do. Luckily, the play's hero _____ comes in to save the day.

Name _____

Commas Around Details

Use proofreading marks to correct the ten errors in capitalization and punctuation in this play review. Make sure every added detail has commas that are placed correctly.

Example: a good play, especially a funny one is a real treat.

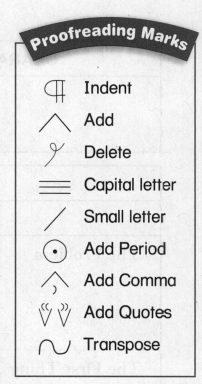

Proofreading Marks

⊬ Indent

∧ Add

⌒ Delete

≡ Capital letter

/ Small letter

⊙ Add Period

∧ Add Comma

ᵛᵛ Add Quotes

∿ Transpose

Last night's play Benny's Big Break, was a delightful surprise. This funny story about Jerome, a new student was smart and fresh. The main actor Roger Lopez said his lines with a sharp sense of humor. all of the actors were terrific? Even Squiggles the family dog, got a lot of laughs

Do you feel like having an hour of pure fun. run to Benny's Big Break and get ready to laugh.

Name _____

Planning a Play

CHARACTERS		SETTING

PLOT
Beginning
The Problem
The First Thing That Happens
Middle
Events
Ending
How Things Turn Out

Name _____

Play Dialogue

Read this paragraph. Part of it has been revised as dialogue in a play. Read and finish the dialogue. Show what the characters are like through what they say. Make them sound like fourth graders.

> Sara meets Matt on the way to school. Sara tells Matt that she has lost her math homework. She is worried about math class. Matt tells Sara that things will probably work out fine. He says that Sara is such a good math student. The teacher will understand.

SARA: Matt! Wait up!

MATT: Hi, Sara. Boy, you look worried. What's up?

SARA: I can't believe it. I lost my math homework! I looked everywhere before I rushed out the door. Where did I put it?

1. MATT: _____

_____

2. SARA: _____

_____

3. MATT: _____

_____

4. SARA: _____

_____

5. MATT: _____

_____

Name _____

Make It Amazing!

Change the underlined words in the paragraph below to make it amazing. The first one is done for you.

When I <u>walked</u> into my <u>house</u> yesterday, I saw <u>my</u> <u>mother</u> on the <u>sofa</u>. She was <u>reading the newspaper</u>. When she <u>looked up</u>, I told her about my day <u>at school</u>.

When I _____*flew*_____ into my _____

yesterday, I saw _____ on the

_____. She was

_____. When she

_____, I told

her about my day _____.

Continue the story to tell about your amazing day!

_____

_____

_____

_____

_____

_____

★ **Bonus** **To make your story even more amazing, rewrite the paragraph, adding adjectives to describe the important nouns. Here are two examples: "my <u>upside down</u> house" and "the <u>floating</u> sofa."**

Name _____

That's Amazing!

	What in the story was realistic?	What amazing things happened in the story?
The Stranger		
Cendrillon		
Heat Wave!		

Which of these stories was most amazing to you? Put a mark
on the line for each story, labeled with the story's title, to show
how realistic you think each one was!

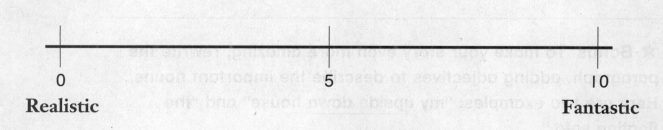

0   5   10

Realistic   **Fantastic**

Name _____

Chilly Crossword

Complete the puzzle using words from the vocabulary list. Write the word that fits each clue.

Across

2. season of year between summer and winter
4. very thin covering of ice
6. an instrument that measures temperature
8. a flow of air

Down

1. strange, odd
3. silvery metal used in thermometers
5. made a design by cutting lines
7. shy; easily frightened

Vocabulary

autumn
draft
etched
frost
mercury
peculiar
thermometer
timid

Name _____

Detail Map

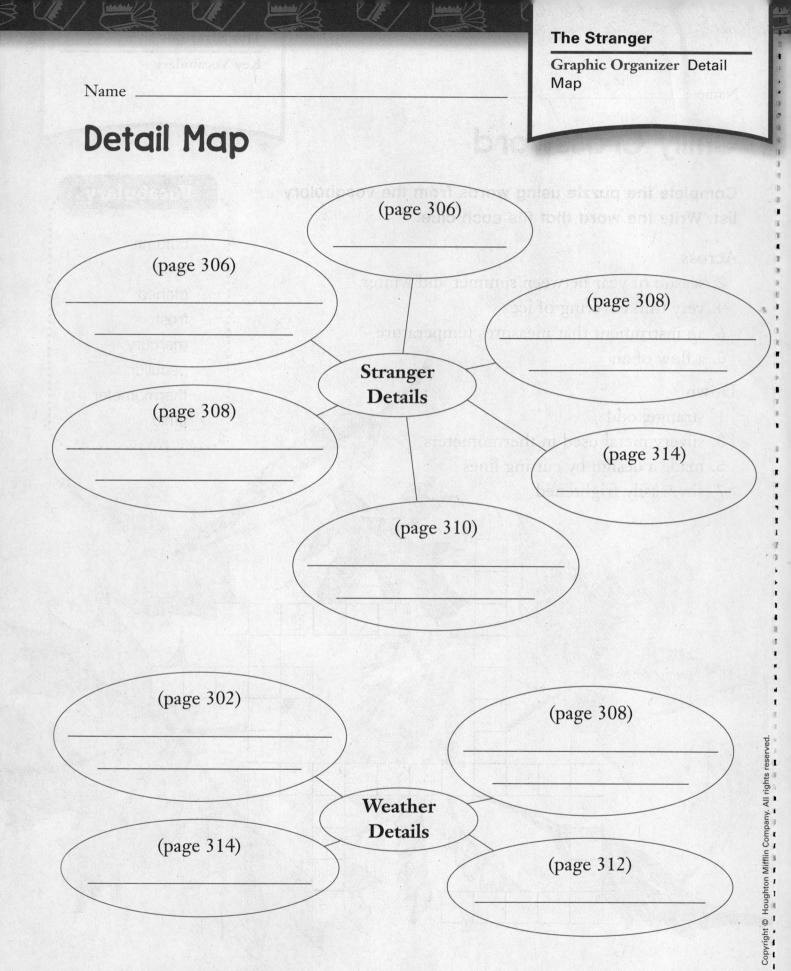

(page 306)
_____

(page 306)
_____
_____

(page 308)
_____
_____

Stranger Details

(page 308)
_____
_____

(page 314)
_____

(page 310)
_____
_____

(page 302)
_____
_____

(page 308)
_____
_____

Weather Details

(page 314)
_____

(page 312)
_____

Name _____

A Nose for Details

Think about the selection. Then answer these questions.

1. What time of year does the story take place?

   _____

2. What happens when Mr. Bailey is driving his truck?

   _____

3. What was the stranger wearing?

   _____

4. What does the stranger **not** do?

   _____

5. The stranger pulls a leaf off a tree and does what?

   _____

6. What happens to the weather and the leaves after the stranger leaves?

   _____

7. What words are etched in frost on the farmhouse windows every year?

   _____

Theme 3: **That's Amazing!**   213

Name _____

Think About It

Read the story. Then complete the detail map on the next page.

What's Your Name?

Mr. Downing's first attempt at a garden since his retirement was a huge disappointment. He had tried everything—plant food, pruning, bug control, and water. It still looked like even the smallest field mouse couldn't get a meal from it.

One day an elderly lady wearing a large hat covered with flowers passed by the fence in front of Mr. Downing's house. She called over to him, "Looks like you could use a little help there." The lady walked over to the garden, tucked her long, curly, gray hair up into her hat, bent down, and immediately began tending the plants.

As Mr. Downing watched her in stunned silence he noticed that the flowers in her hat were real. "How odd," he thought. Then he heard the lady softly talking. He was about to ask her to speak up when he realized she wasn't talking to him but the plants instead.

Mr. Downing focused his eyes on the lady for quite some time. Finally she stood up and spoke to him. "Remember, a little conversation never hurts." She began to walk away.

A little confused, Mr. Downing looked from her to his garden. He was amazed at the sight before his eyes. The flowers were blooming and there were vegetables on the vines. He turned back, thanked the lady and asked her name.

"Everybody just calls me Mother," she said, with a smile full of sunshine.

Name _____

Think About It

Complete this Detail Map for the story "What's Your Name?"

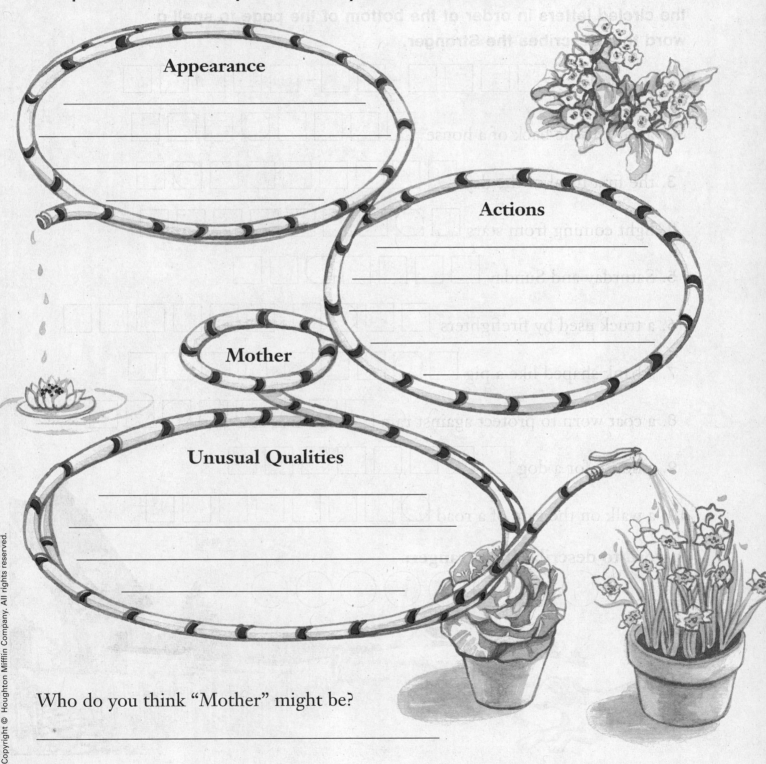

Appearance

_____

_____

_____

Actions

_____

_____

_____

Mother

Unusual Qualities

_____

_____

_____

Who do you think "Mother" might be?

_____

Name _____

Compound Challenge

Write the compound word that matches each clue. Then write the circled letters in order at the bottom of the page to spell a word that describes the Stranger.

1. carousel ☐☐☐☐☐ - ☐☐ - ☐☐☐☐☐☐

2. a yard at the back of a house ☐☐☐☐☐☐☐☐

3. the first meal of the day ☐☐☐☐☐☐☐☐☐

4. light coming from stars ☐☐☐☐☐☐☐☐☐

5. Saturday and Sunday ☐☐☐☐☐☐☐

6. a truck used by firefighters ☐☐☐☐☐☐☐☐☐

7. a bank shaped like a pig ☐☐☐☐☐☐☐☐☐

8. a coat worn to protect against rain ☐☐☐☐☐☐☐☐

9. a house for a dog ☐☐☐☐☐☐☐☐

10. a walk on the side of a road ☐☐☐☐☐☐☐☐

A word to describe the Stranger:

◯ ◯ ◯ ◯ ◯ ◯ ◯ ◯ ◯ ◯

Name _____

Compound Words

A **compound word** is made up of two or more smaller words. To spell a compound word correctly, you must know if it is written as one word, as two words joined by a hyphen, or as two separate words.

rail + **road** = railroad   **ninety** + **nine** = ninety-nine

seat + **belt** = seat belt

► In the starred word *already*, an *l* was dropped in *all* to make one word.

Write each Spelling Word under the heading that tells how the word is written.

Spelling Words

1. railroad
2. airport
3. seat belt
4. everywhere
5. homesick
6. understand
7. background
8. anything
9. ninety-nine
10. already*
11. fireplace
12. ourselves
13. all right
14. forever
15. breakfast
16. whenever
17. everything
18. meanwhile
19. afternoon
20. make-believe

One Word

_____   _____

_____   _____

_____   _____

_____   _____

_____   _____

_____   _____

With a Hyphen   **Two Words**

_____   _____

_____   _____

Name _____

Spelling Spree

What Am I? Write the Spelling Word that answers each riddle.

1. I'm cereal and juice, and I happen before lunch.

   What am I? _____

2. I'm really quite old, but less than one hundred.

   What am I? _____

3. I'm the part of the day between morning and night.

   What am I? _____

4. Fasten me and I'll save you from crashes.

   What am I? _____

5. If going by plane, you must pass through me.

   What am I? _____

Finish the word Each of the words below forms part of a Spelling Word. Write the Spelling Words on the lines.

6. any _____

7. home _____

8. under _____

9. back _____

10. where _____

11. our _____

12. all _____

13. when _____

14. while _____

15. believe _____

Spelling Words

1. railroad
2. airport
3. seat belt
4. everywhere
5. homesick
6. understand
7. background
8. anything
9. ninety-nine
10. already*
11. fireplace
12. ourselves
13. all right
14. forever
15. breakfast
16. whenever
17. everything
18. meanwhile
19. afternoon
20. make-believe

218   Theme 3: **That's Amazing!**

Name _____

Proofreading and Writing

Proofreading   Circle the five misspelled Spelling Words in the newspaper article. Then write each word correctly.

Spelling Words

Weird Weather Grips Town

Up until two days ago, everyone was enjoying the warm fall weather. Local farmers reported that everthing was still growing at an amazing rate. Enormous pumpkins had allready been harvested. Then winter arrived without notice. Experts are predicting snow that may cause railrode and airport delays. Weather reporter Storm Sky says the cold snap won't last foreever. Stay indoors today, though. This is the perfect time to curl up by the firplace with a good book.

1. railroad
2. airport
3. seat belt
4. everywhere
5. homesick
6. understand
7. background
8. anything
9. ninety-nine
10. already*
11. fireplace
12. ourselves
13. all right
14. forever
15. breakfast
16. whenever
17. everything
18. meanwhile
19. afternoon
20. make-believe

1. _____   4. _____

2. _____   5. _____

3. _____

✏️ **Write Helpful Hints** The stranger in the story was unfamiliar with many things in the Bailey house. Have you ever helped a person in an unfamiliar situation? What information would be helpful to that person?

On a separate sheet of paper, write a list of helpful tips for newcomers to your town or neighborhood. You might include information such as where to get the best pizza. Use Spelling Words from the list.

Name _____

Strange Synonyms

Suppose that the Baileys have a neighbor, and the neighbor wrote this letter to a cousin. She uses the word *strange* in almost every sentence. From the word list, choose synonyms to add variety to the letter. Some of the words are exact synonyms for *strange*, while others give a better sense of the sentence. Some words will fit in more than one sentence, but use each word only once. Use the sentence context to help decide which words fit best.

Dear Cousin Joe,

Our town had a very 1. strange autumn. Every leaf stayed green for weeks, which is 2. strange for these parts. A 3. strange wind blew in the trees, making it feel just like summer. Everyone noticed the 4. strange weather, even the new person in town. He was a little 5. strange — he didn't talk much, but he sure could play the fiddle! He had a 6. strange gift with animals. But the weather must have been too 7. strange for him, because he left suddenly. The town felt 8. strange without him. We missed him a lot. Shortly after he left, the 9. strange summer weather turned to fall. It's too bad that the 10. strange stranger left so soon. I think he would have liked autumn.

Your cousin,

Freda

Vocabulary

unusual

shy

unique

warm

unknown

rare

unfamiliar

new

odd

special

cool

weird

sad

uncommon

timid

quiet

different

lonely

1. _____   6. _____

2. _____   7. _____

3. _____   8. _____

4. _____   9. _____

5. _____   10. _____

Name _____

Letter with Action Verbs

What if Katy Bailey had a cousin and she wrote a letter to him? Read the letter. Circle each action verb and write it on the lines below.

Dear Cousin,

We have a new guest at our house. I think he lives in the forest near us. He wears a leather shirt and pants. His breath makes things cold. I call him "Jack Frost." He likes my mother's cooking, though. He especially enjoys her homemade vegetable soup. I hope you meet him soon.

Love,

Katy

_____   _____

_____   _____

_____   _____

_____   _____

Name _____

Take Action!

Suppose Katy tells her class about the stranger who came to stay with her family. Complete Katy's story by filling each blank with an action verb. Choose verbs from the box or use action verbs of your own.

> change
> disappears
> drives
> grows
> hears
> jams
> helps
> jumps
> listens
> works

One fall day as my father _____ his truck along the road, he _____ a loud thump. He _____ on the brakes and _____ out of the truck. Father _____ the stranger into his truck.

The doctor _____ to the stranger's heart. The stranger _____ stronger and _____ with Father on the farm. When the stranger _____, the leaves _____ color and the weather turns cold.

Name _____

Using Action Verbs

Using Exact Verbs Good writers use verbs that name specific actions to produce a vivid image in the reader's mind. Read each sentence below. Then rewrite the sentence. Substitute an exact verb for the general word or phrase in parentheses.

1. The doctor (looks at) the man's body.

    _____

2. The doctor (finds) a lump on the man's head.

    _____

3. The stranger (does the same thing as) Katy as she cools her soup.

    _____

4. The cold breath (makes) a chill up Mrs. Bailey's spine.

    _____

5. The rabbits do not (act frightened by) the stranger.

    _____

6. The stranger (goes) along when Mr. Bailey works in the fields.

    _____

7. Two weeks (go by) and the stranger can't remember his name.

    _____

8. The stranger (wondered about) the colors of the leaves on the trees.

    _____

Name _____

Writing an Explanation

Use this page to plan your explanation. You can explain why something happens or how something happens. Then number your reasons or facts in the order you will use them.

Topic:
Title:

Topic Sentence:

Reason / Fact:	Reason / Fact:

Reason / Fact:	Reason / Fact:

Name _____

Audience

Writers are always aware of their audience. A good writer will adapt the style of writing to fit the reader.

► Formal writing is used for reports, presentations, many school assignments, and business letters.

> **Formal:** Deer can be found in almost all regions of the United States. Although they are wild animals, they can become quite used to the presence of human beings.

► Informal writing is for friendly letters, postcards, or e-mails between friends.

> **Informal:** We saw the most incredible deer today. I was careful to walk up to it really slowly. I stretched out my hand, and it sniffed my palm. It felt really funny!

Write two short paragraphs about the change of seasons. Make the first one formal, as if you were giving a report. Make the second one informal, as if you were writing a postcard to a good friend.

The Change of Seasons

Formal:

_____

_____

_____

_____

Informal:

_____

_____

_____

_____

Name _____

Revising Your Story

Reread your story. Put a checkmark in the box for each sentence that describes your paper. Use this page to help you revise.

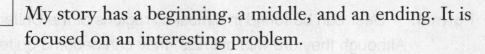

Rings the Bell

☐ My story has a beginning, a middle, and an ending. It is focused on an interesting problem.

☐ Detail and dialogue make characters seem real.

☐ I wrote in a way that will get my reader's attention.

☐ Many exact words create vivid pictures.

☐ Sentences flow smoothly, and there are few mistakes.

Getting Stronger

☐ My beginning, middle, or ending is weak. The problem could be more interesting.

☐ I need more details and dialogue for my characters.

☐ My writing won't always hold my reader's attention.

☐ My words are vague. I could make them more exact.

☐ Some sentences are choppy. There are a few mistakes.

Try Harder

☐ There is no beginning, middle, ending, or problem.

☐ I didn't use any details. There is no dialogue.

☐ My writing sounds flat.

☐ I use the same word many times.

☐ Most sentences are choppy. There are many mistakes.

Name _____

Using Possessives

A **possessive** shows ownership.
► Add **'s** to make nouns possessive.
► For plurals that end in *s*, add an apostrophe.

Rewrite each phrase, using a possessive noun. Then use the new phrase in a sentence of your own.

1. the pouch of the kangaroo _____

_____

_____

2. the roar of the lion _____

_____

_____

3. the buzz of the flies _____

_____

_____

4. the cleverness of the foxes _____

_____

_____

5. the prey belonging to the tiger _____

_____

_____

6. the symphony of the frogs _____

_____

_____

Spelling Words

Words Often Misspelled Look for familiar spelling patterns to help you remember how to spell the Spelling Words on this page. Think carefully about the parts that you find hard to spell in each word.

Write the missing letters in the Spelling Words below.

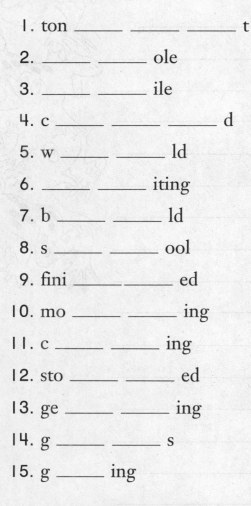

1. ton _____ _____ _____ t
2. _____ _____ ole
3. _____ _____ ile
4. c _____ _____ _____ d
5. w _____ _____ ld
6. _____ _____ iting
7. b _____ _____ ld
8. s _____ _____ ool
9. fini _____ _____ ed
10. mo _____ _____ ing
11. c _____ _____ ing
12. sto _____ _____ ed
13. ge _____ _____ ing
14. g _____ _____ s
15. g _____ ing

1. tonight
2. whole
3. while
4. could
5. world
6. writing
7. build
8. school
9. finished
10. morning
11. coming
12. stopped
13. getting
14. goes
15. going

Study List On a separate piece of paper, write each Spelling Word. Check your spelling against the words on the list.

Spelling Spree

Write a Spelling Word to fit each clue.

1. a word meaning "at the same time as" _____
2. a two-syllable synonym for *done* _____
3. the opposite of *going* _____
4. a pencil helps you with this _____
5. what the car did at the red light _____
6. the whole wide _____
7. a synonym for *leaving* _____
8. what carpenters do _____
9. a place for learning _____
10. not broken into smaller pieces _____

Word Addition Combine the first part of the first word with the second part of the second word to write a Spelling Word.

11. goat + sees   _____
12. couch + mold   _____
13. tons + light   _____
14. more + inning   _____
15. germ + sitting   _____

Spelling Words

1. tonight
2. whole
3. while
4. could
5. world
6. writing
7. build
8. school
9. finished
10. morning
11. coming
12. stopped
13. getting
14. goes
15. going

Theme 3: **That's Amazing!**   229

Proofreading and Writing

Proofreading Circle the five misspelled Spelling Words in this newspaper item. Then write each word correctly.

The latest episode of *Amazing and Incredible* will be on tonigt at eight o'clock. It coud be an interesting program. Most of the show is about a woman who tried to build a house out of old soft drink bottles. Apparently, she finnished most of two stories. However, she stoped when she realized that the bottles wouldn't be able to support a roof. There will also be an interview with a person who's trying to row a boat around the werld. This show can be seen on Channel 9.

Spelling Words

1. tonight
2. whole
3. while
4. could
5. world
6. writing
7. build
8. school
9. finished
10. morning
11. coming
12. stopped
13. getting
14. goes
15. going

1. _____

2. _____

3. _____

4. _____

5. _____

Rhyming Sentences Pick five Spelling Words from the list. Then write a sentence for each word. In each sentence, include a word that rhymes with the Spelling Word. Underline the rhyming words.

Name _____

A Perfect Match

Write the letter to match each word with its definition.

_____ **crossly**

_____ **elegant**

_____ **godmother**

_____ **orphan**

_____ **peasant**

_____ **proud**

a. a woman who acts as a sponsor at a child's christening

b. a poor farm worker

c. thinking too highly of oneself

d. in a grumpy or grouchy way

e. a child whose parents are dead

f. marked by good taste; graceful

Write your own sentence for each vocabulary word.

1. orphan: _____

_____

2. godmother: _____

_____

3. elegant: _____

_____

4. proud: _____

_____

5. crossly: _____

_____

6. peasant: _____

_____

Name _____

Venn Diagram

Vitaline and Cendrillon

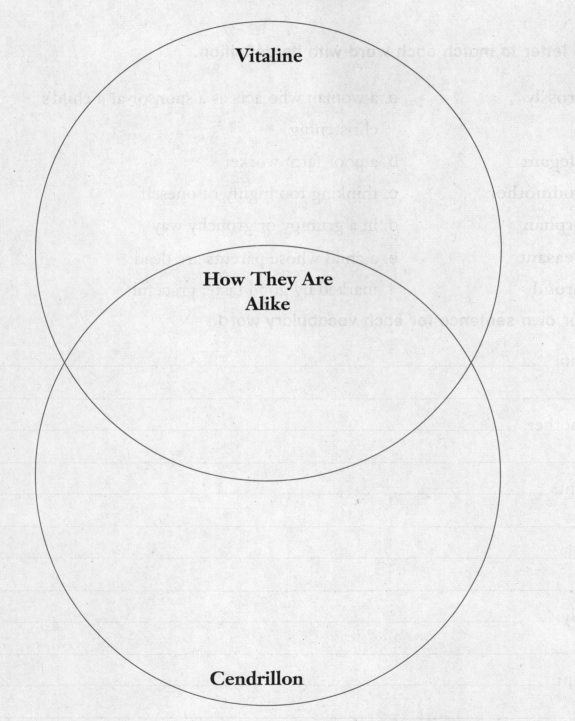

Vitaline

How They Are Alike

Cendrillon

Name _____

Memory Check

Think about the selection. Then complete the sentences.

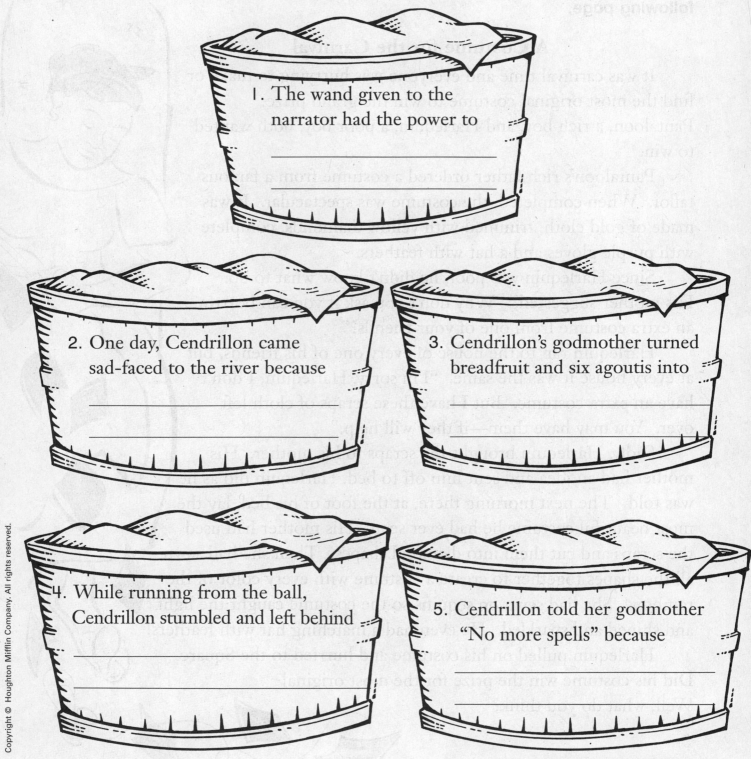

1. The wand given to the narrator had the power to
_____
_____

2. One day, Cendrillon came sad-faced to the river because
_____
_____

3. Cendrillon's godmother turned breadfruit and six agoutis into
_____
_____

4. While running from the ball, Cendrillon stumbled and left behind
_____
_____

5. Cendrillon told her godmother "No more spells" because
_____
_____

Name _____

A Resourceful Parent

Read the story. Then complete the Venn diagram on the following page.

A Costume for the Carnival

It was carnival time and everyone was hurrying to make or find the most original costume to win the grand prize. Pantaloon, a rich boy, and Harlequin, a poor boy, both wanted to win.

Pantaloon's rich father ordered a costume from a famous tailor. When completed, the costume was spectacular. It was made of gold cloth, trimmed with yellow diamonds, complete with purple gloves and a hat with feathers.

Since Harlequin was poor, he didn't know what to do. His mother suggested, "Why don't you ask if you can borrow an extra costume from one of your friends?"

Harlequin ran to the house of every one of his friends, but at every house it was the same. "I'm sorry, Harlequin, I don't have an extra costume. But I have these scraps of cloth left over. You may have them—if they will help."

Sadly, Harlequin brought the scraps to his mother. His mother had an idea and sent him off to bed. Harlequin did as he was told. The next morning there, at the foot of his bed, lay the most beautiful costume he had ever seen! His mother had used the scraps and cut them into diamond shapes. Then she had sewn all the shapes together to create a costume with every color of the rainbow! She had sewn on sequins so the costume caught the light and shined and sparkled. He even had a matching hat with feathers!

Harlequin pulled on his costume and hurried to the Square. Did his costume win the prize for the most original? Well, what do you think?

Name _____

A Resourceful Parent continued

Complete the Venn Diagram for the story "A Costume for the Carnival."

Harlequin's Costume

1. _____
2. _____
3. _____

How the Costumes are Alike

1. _____
2. _____

Pantaloon's Costume

1. _____
2. _____
3. _____

If you were one of the costume judges, would you award the prize to Harlequin or Pantaloon? Why? Use complete sentences.

_____

_____

_____

Name _____

A Suffix Story

Fill in each blank with a word from the box and the suffix
***-able*. Then finish the fairy tale by writing what happens
next. Try to use at least one word with the suffix *-able* in
your story ending.**

    Once upon a time, Angelina was given a magic wand
by her fairy godmother. This magic wand was the most
marvelous thing _____. It could
make a hard wooden chair _____.
It could make the most difficult book
_____. One wave of the wand, and
an old game became _____. or a
shirt that was too small became _____
again. Even a lost jewel or a tiny charm became
_____.

    But one day, the _____ wand
disappeared! Angelina looked everywhere. Finally she cried,
"This is not _____! Where is my
wand?" Was the problem _____?

_____

_____

_____

_____

_____

Name _____

Final /ər/ and Final /l/ or /əl/

A syllable is a word or word part that has one vowel sound. The final syllable of some words ends with a weak vowel sound + r or l. This weak vowel sound is called **schwa** and is shown as /ə/. When you hear the final /ər/ sounds in a two-syllable word, think of the patterns er, or, and ar. When you hear the final /l/ or /əl/ sounds in a two-syllable word, think of the patterns el, al, and le.

final /ər/   er, or, ar (weath**er**, harb**or**, sug**ar**)

final /l/ or /əl/   el, al, le (mod**el**, fin**al**, mid**dle**)

Write each Spelling Word under its spelling of the final /ər/, /l/, or /əl/ sounds.

Spelling Words

1. harbor
2. final
3. middle
4. weather
5. labor
6. model
7. chapter
8. special
9. sugar
10. bottle
11. medal
12. collar
13. proper
14. towel
15. beggar
16. battle
17. trouble
18. shower
19. uncle
20. doctor

er

_____
_____
_____

or

_____
_____

ar

_____
_____

el

_____
_____

al

_____
_____

le

_____
_____
_____

Name _____

Spelling Spree

Crossword Use the Spelling Words from the box to complete the crossword puzzle.

Across

2. a brother of your mother or father
4. cloth used to dry things
7. unusual or exceptional
8. polite
9. home for a boat
11. a small copy
13. a brief rain
14. work

Down

1. container for liquids
3. part of a shirt
5. a section of a book
6. rain, sun, or snow
10. someone who begs
12. someone who practices medicine
13. a substance used to sweeten food

Spelling Words

1. harbor
2. final
3. middle
4. weather
5. labor
6. model
7. chapter
8. special
9. sugar
10. bottle
11. medal
12. collar
13. proper
14. towel
15. beggar
16. battle
17. trouble
18. shower
19. uncle
20. doctor

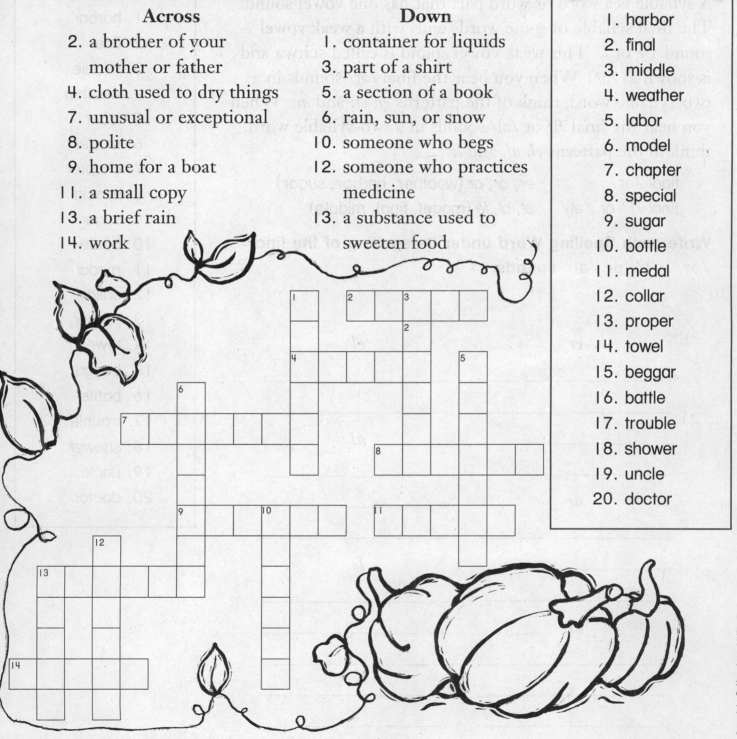

Proofreading and Writing

Proofreading Circle the five misspelled Spelling Words in this diary entry. Then write each word correctly.

Spelling Words

Dear Diary,

It was a battel against all odds, but I got to the ball after all! Nannin' helped me with her special wand. She deserves a medle for her efforts. I looked so fine in my blue velvet gown and pink slippers. Alas, right in the middel of the ball, everything went wrong. Nannin' said we would be in truble if we didn't leave right away. Then I stumbled and lost one of my slippers. By the finel stroke of midnight my gown had turned to rags. All I have left is one slipper. I am determined to find the other one, even if I have to knock on every door in town!

1. harbor
2. final
3. middle
4. weather
5. labor
6. model
7. chapter
8. special
9. sugar
10. bottle
11. medal
12. collar
13. proper
14. towel
15. beggar
16. battle
17. trouble
18. shower
19. uncle
20. doctor

1. _____ 4. _____

2. _____ 5. _____

3. _____

✏ **Write an Explanation** Think about *Cendrillon* and other fairy tales you have read. What do you like about these stories? Are there things about fairy tales that you don't like?

On a separate sheet of paper, write a paragraph giving reasons why you like or dislike fairy tales. Use some of the Spelling Words from the list.

Name _____

Make a Spelling Table Pronunciation Key

Write the words in the correct blanks to complete the spelling table/pronunciation key below. Then underline the letters in those words that match the sound.

wand	fruit	chime
coach	round	guests
lost	spoil	gasp
blaze	scarf	stood

Spelling Table / Pronunciation Key	
Sound	**Sample Words**
/ă/	hand, _____
/ā/	face, _____
/ä/	march, _____
/ĕ/	bread, _____
/ī/	my, _____
/ŏ/	hot, _____
/ō/	most, _____
/ô/	fall, _____
oi	boy, _____
/o͝o/	cook, _____
/o͞o/	move, _____
ou	crowd, _____

Name _____

Identifying Verbs

Underline the whole verb in each sentence. Then write the main verb and the helping verb on the lines below.

1. Cendrillon's stepmother has made the girl a servant.

   Main verb: _____

   Helping verb: _____

2. Cendrillon and her godmother have washed clothes at the river.

   Main verb: _____

   Helping verb: _____

3. Cendrillon has suffered without complaint.

   Main verb: _____

   Helping verb: _____

4. Who has arrived at the ball?

   Main verb: _____

   Helping verb: _____

5. Her godmother has accompanied her to the ball.

   Main verb: _____

   Helping verb: _____

Name _____

Writing Helping Verbs

**Change each verb in the sentences below by adding *has* or
have. Write the new sentence on the lines.**

1. Cendrillon's stepmother scolded her.

_____

_____

2. Cendrillon and her godmother washed clothes for the family.

_____

_____

3. The godmother changed the agoutis into horses.

_____

_____

4. The carriage traveled over the bridge.

_____

_____

5. Cendrillon and the handsome young man danced all evening.

_____

_____

Name _____

Using Helping Verbs

Good writers often combine two sentences that have the same subject and helping verb but different main verbs. Read each pair of sentences below. Then rewrite the two sentences as one sentence by combining the main verbs and helping verbs. Write your new sentence on the lines provided.

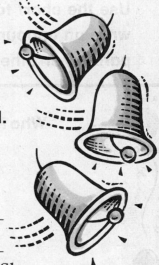

1. Cendrillon's godmother has tapped the breadfruit with her wand. She has turned it into a gilded coach.

   _____

   _____

2. The godmother has turned the agoutis into carriage horses. She has changed the lizards into tall footmen.

   _____

   _____

3. The carriage has crossed the bridge. The carriage has arrived at the mansion.

   _____

   _____

4. All the guests have looked at Cendrillon. They have talked about her.

   _____

   _____

5. Cendrillon has heard the bells. She has run from the ball.

   _____

   _____

Name _____

Writing an Announcement

Use the chart to organize your ideas for an announcement. Then
write an announcement about a birth, wedding, concert, fair,
parade, or other special event.

Who?	What?	Where?
When?	Why?	How?

_____

_____

_____

_____

_____

_____

_____

Name _____

Ordering Important Information

► When writing an announcement, first decide what information is most important. Put that information first.
► Put other information in order of importance from most important to least important.
► Be sure your announcement includes all the necessary information that answers some or all of these questions: who, what, where, when, why, how.

Use the following outline to write a wedding announcement for Cendrillon and Paul. Fill in the information in the outline. Then put the information in the order that makes the most sense.

Where will it take place?

_____

What is the occasion?

_____

What time?

_____

When will it take place?

_____

Who is the announcement about?

_____

_____

_____

_____

_____

Name _____

What Do You Mean?

Write the word from the box that fits each definition.

Vocabulary

affected
horizon
miscalculated
singe
temperature
weather vane

1. to burn slightly

_____

2. moveable pointer that shows wind direction

_____

3. figured incorrectly

_____

4. measure of heat or coldness

_____

5. the line along which the sky and the earth seem to meet

_____

6. caused a change in

_____

**Write the word from the vocabulary list that belongs
in each group.**

7. Words about fire

   burn   char   scorch _____

8. Words that tell about making mistakes

   misspelled   misjudged   mistaken _____

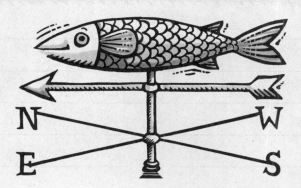

Fantasy/Realism Chart

Page	Story Detail	Fantasy (F)/ Realism (R)
361		
367		
368		
371		
375		

Name _____

That's Fantastic! continued

**Complete this chart for the story "The Big Little Machine." Label
the details with an F if it's *fantasy* or R if it is *realism*. Write in
other details when the letter F or R is provided for you.**

Story Detail	Fantasy (F) or Realism (R)?
golf clubs becoming toothpicks	
sister's clothes fitting her doll	
	R
having a family meeting to solve a problem	
	R
Gruffly, the dog, chasing the cat	
	F
	F

Name _____

Add the Ending

► When a base word ends with *e*, the *e* is dropped
before adding *-ed* or *-ing*.   *move/moved/moving*

► When a base word ends with one vowel followed by
a single consonant, the consonant is doubled before
adding *-ed* or *-ing*.   *pop/popped/popping*

**Read each sentence. Choose a word from the box
similar in meaning to the word or words in dark type.
Complete the puzzle by adding *-ed* or *-ing* to your word.**

| turn |
| rise |
| bake |
| stir |
| race |
| drive |
| switch |
| grab |
| hop |
| scrub |

Across

1. My brother **changed** his tune when the Heat Wave hit.
4. Pa started **washing** the cows as hard as he could.
6. The cows were **jumping** around like rabbits.
7. The dough was **going up** so fast we ran for our lives.
8. We **hurried** into the barn, but it was too late.
9. I **snatched** a shovel and ran to the cornfield.

Down

2. Ma was **steering** the truck out to the cornfield.
3. We watched the Heat Wave **twisting** in the sky.
4. I **mixed** the water and the flour in a trough.
5. The dough **cooked** in the heat.

Words with *-ed* or *-ing*

Each of these words has a base word and an ending. A **base word** is a word to which a beginning or an ending can be added. If a word ends with *e*, drop the *e* before adding *-ed* or *-ing*. If a one-syllable word ends with one vowel followed by a single consonant, double the consonant before adding *-ed* or *-ing*.

race + **ed** = rac**ed**　　　land + **ed** = land**ed**

snap + **ing** = sna**pping**

Write each Spelling Word under the heading that tells what happens to its spelling when *-ed* or *-ing* is added.

Spelling Words

1. dancing
2. skipped
3. hiking
4. flipped
5. snapping
6. raced
7. landed
8. pleasing
9. checking
10. dared
11. dimmed
12. rubbing
13. striped
14. wasting
15. traced
16. stripped
17. tanning
18. smelling
19. phoning
20. fainted

No Spelling Change

_____

_____

_____

_____

Final Consonant Doubled

_____

_____

_____

_____

_____

_____

Final *e* Dropped

_____

_____

_____

_____

_____

_____

Name _____

Spelling Spree

joke top

care wrap

joking topping

wrapped cared

Word Factory Write Spelling Words by adding *-ed* or *-ing* to each word below.

1. flip _____
2. please _____
3. land _____
4. stripe _____
5. check _____
6. trace _____
7. rub _____
8. tan _____
9. strip _____

Meaning Match Write a Spelling Word that has each meaning and ending below.

Example: repair + ing *fixing*

10. pass out + ed _____
11. detect an odor + ing _____
12. run at top speed + ed _____
13. go on a long walk + ing _____
14. challenge someone + ed _____
15. make a cracking sound + ing _____

Spelling Words

1. dancing
2. skipped
3. hiking
4. flipped
5. snapping
6. raced
7. landed
8. pleasing
9. checking
10. dared
11. dimmed
12. rubbing
13. striped
14. wasting
15. traced
16. stripped
17. tanning
18. smelling
19. phoning
20. fainted

Name _____

Proofreading and Writing

Proofreading Circle the five misspelled Spelling Words in the following memo. Then write each word correctly.

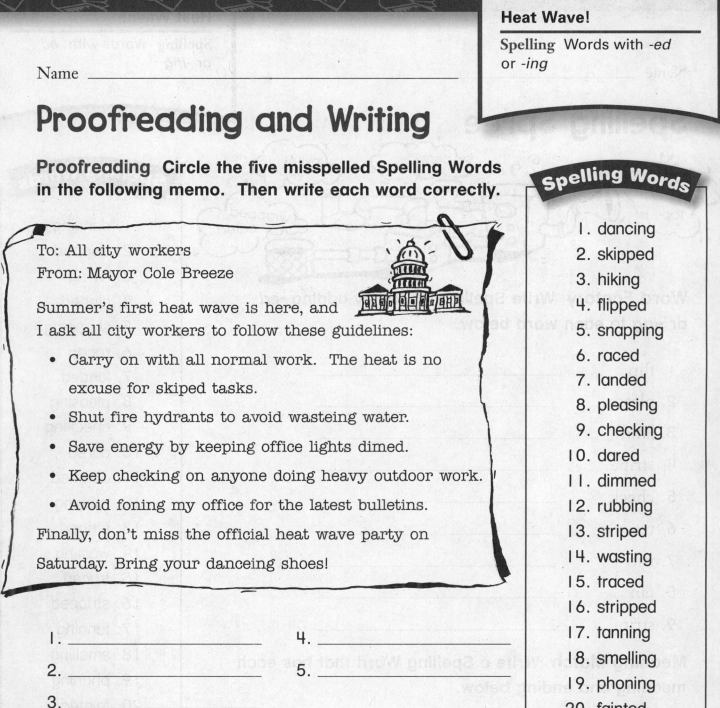

To: All city workers
From: Mayor Cole Breeze

Summer's first heat wave is here, and
I ask all city workers to follow these guidelines:

- Carry on with all normal work. The heat is no excuse for skiped tasks.
- Shut fire hydrants to avoid wasteing water.
- Save energy by keeping office lights dimed.
- Keep checking on anyone doing heavy outdoor work.
- Avoid foning my office for the latest bulletins.

Finally, don't miss the official heat wave party on
Saturday. Bring your danceing shoes!

1. _____   4. _____
2. _____   5. _____
3. _____

Spelling Words

1. dancing
2. skipped
3. hiking
4. flipped
5. snapping
6. raced
7. landed
8. pleasing
9. checking
10. dared
11. dimmed
12. rubbing
13. striped
14. wasting
15. traced
16. stripped
17. tanning
18. smelling
19. phoning
20. fainted

✏️ **Write a Funny Weather Report** Have you ever experienced a long period of hot or cold weather, snow, or heavy rain? Try to remember what it was like. Then imagine what might happen if the weather's effects were greatly exaggerated.

On a separate sheet of paper, write a funny weather report predicting severe weather. Use Spelling Words from the list.

Name _____

Divide and Conquer

Here are sixteen words from *Heat Wave!* Divide each word into syllables. Then write each word in the correct column on the chart below.

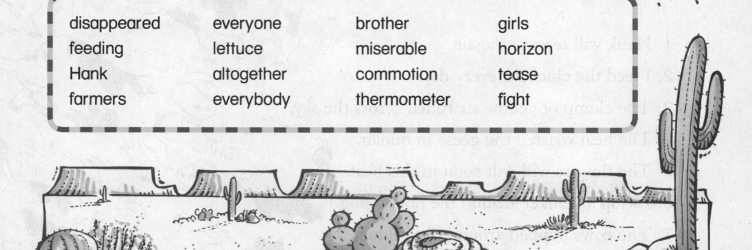

disappeared	everyone	brother	girls
feeding	lettuce	miserable	horizon
Hank	altogether	commotion	tease
farmers	everybody	thermometer	fight

Words with One Syllable

_____

_____

_____

Words with Two Syllables

_____

_____

_____

Words with Three Syllables

_____

_____

_____

Words with Four Syllables

_____

_____

_____

Getting the Tense

Underline the verb in each sentence. Then write each verb in the correct column, under *Present Tense*, *Past Tense*, or *Future Tense*.

1. Hank will tease me again.
2. I feed the chickens every day.
3. The clump of yellow air rolled across the sky.
4. The heat roasted the geese in midair.
5. The flowers will wilt soon in this heat.
6. I wrap a blanket around the hound dog.
7. The cows hopped around like rabbits.
8. The cows' milk will turn to butter.
9. We pour butter over the popcorn.
10. The oats dried in the field.

Present Tense	Past Tense	Future Tense
_____	_____	_____
_____	_____	_____
_____	_____	_____
	_____	

Name _____

Reporting in the Past Tense

Help the reporter complete the news story by writing the correct past-tense forms of the verbs in parentheses.

Last week an unusual thing _____.

(happen) We _____ a very sudden heat

wave. (suffer) No one quite _____ the

temperature. (believe) The mercury just

_____ out of the thermometer at one

farm here. (blast) The ground was so hot, cows

_____ up and down. (jump) Their

movements _____ their milk to butter.

(turn) The farmer's daughter _____ the

hot cows down and _____ them. (hose)

(cool) She _____ wetting down the oats

but she only _____ a huge, lumpy field

of oatmeal. (try) (create) If you have any other stories about

the heat wave, call the newspaper immediately.

Write three sentences of your own about the heat wave, using past tense verbs.

_____

_____

_____

Name _____

Using the Correct Tense

Good writers make sure to choose the verb tense that correctly shows the time of the action described. Read the diary entry that the girl in the story might have written. Rewrite it so that all of the verbs show that the events have already happened.

> Dear Diary,
>   Yesterday begins like a normal day. It turns out to be a strange day. It will start with a hot wind blowing in. The wind sounds like the roar of a lion. The wind quickly heats up everything.
>   This wind created lots of trouble. It nearly burns all the crops. We save the popcorn, though. At one point, I almost will drown in oatmeal. Finally, some crows flap their wings and cool us off.

_____

_____

_____

_____

_____

_____

_____

_____

Name _____

Writing a Summary

Use this page to plan a summary of the first few pages of _Heat Wave!_ Write the main idea for the story in the top box. Then write an important detail for each page of the story.

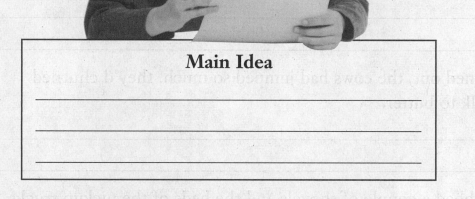

Main Idea
_____
_____
_____

Page 361 Detail
_____
_____
_____

Page 363 Detail
_____
_____
_____

Page 365 Detail
_____
_____
_____

Name _____

Paraphrasing

► Writers use paraphrasing when they write a summary or
notes for a report.

► Paraphrasing is restating an idea in your own words,
without changing the author's meaning.

"Then we heard a commotion in the pasture."

Which paraphrasing does not change the author's meaning?

☑ Then we heard noise coming from the pasture.

☐ Then we saw something in the pasture.

Paraphrase each sentence.

1. The ground had gotten too hot, so we herded the cows inside the barn.

_____

_____

2. As it turned out, the cows had jumped so much, they'd churned
their milk to butter.

_____

_____

3. We scrubbed a couple of shovels and the beds of the pickup trucks.

_____

_____

4. I sent Pa and Hank to the field to fill the pickups with popcorn.

_____

_____

5. In no time at all, they sold every last bit of that popcorn, then hurried home.

_____

_____

Name _____

Make a Match

Match each word to its definition by writing the letter on the line beside the word. Then write your own sentence for each vocabulary word.

I. _____ turmoil   a. poked out from something

2. _____ object   b. unusual

3. _____ curious   c. a state of confusion

4. _____ draught   d. a thing you can feel or see

5. _____ protruded   e. flowing air

6. curious

_____

7. protruded

_____

8. turmoil

_____

9. object

_____

10. draught

_____

Name _____

Is It Real?

Write down four amazing details from each story. Then label each as real (R) or fantasy (F).

	Amazing Detail or Event	Real or Fantasy?
The Borrowers		
Lord of the Fleas		

"Real life is stranger than fiction." After reading *The Borrowers* and "Lord of the Fleas," do you agree with this statement? Why or why not?

_____

_____

_____

Name _____

Getting the Big Picture

Think about *The Borrowers*. Then read the paragraph below. Pay attention to each underlined detail. If it is correct, write *OK*. If it is incorrect, write the correct detail on the line.

I finally got to meet the rest of the <u>little</u> _____ family that lives in our house. I used a <u>hammer</u> _____ to pry up the floorboard above where they live. The one named Homily <u>screamed</u> _____ when I did it, which I wasn't expecting. I asked Arietty, and she said Homily was her <u>father</u>. _____ I gave them all a <u>table</u> _____ to use in their house. I hope I get another chance to talk to them soon.

Name _____

Test Practice continued

2. **Connecting/Comparing** Compare what the girl does to help animals in *Heat Wave!* with what Hans Mathes does to fleas in *Lord of the Fleas.* Do you think that what Hans Mathes does is cruel? Explain your reasoning.

_____

_____

_____

_____

_____

_____

_____

_____

_____

_____

_____

_____

_____

_____

Checklist for Writing a Personal Response

✔ Did I restate the question at the beginning?

✔ Can I add more details from what I read to support my answer?

✔ Can I add more of my thoughts, feelings, or experiences to support my answer?

✔ Do I need to delete details that do not help answer the question?

✔ Where can I add more exact words?

✔ Did I use clear handwriting? Did I make any mistakes?

Read your answers aloud to a partner. Then discuss the checklist. Make any changes that will improve your answers.

Read for Details

**Reread pages 382–383 of *The Borrowers*. Pay careful attention
to the author's description of the dresser the human boy gives
the Clock family. Write the details you notice on the lines below.**

_____

_____

_____

**Write *T* by each detail that is true about the dresser. Write *F* for
each detail that is not true.**

1. was originally made for a doll _____

2. has four drawers _____

3. has two cupboards above the drawers _____

4. is made of dark oak _____

5. has hand-painted plates _____

6. has drawers that don't open _____

Name _____

Compare Flea Performers

**Read the paragraphs. Then fill in the Venn diagram to show
likenesses and differences.**

> Hans Mathes picks fleas for his circus carefully. He chooses only
> females, and he prefers fleas that live on humans rather than fleas
> that live on animals. All of the fleas he chooses are strong.
>
> After choosing the fleas, he sorts them into two groups. All
> fleas are natural jumpers, but some like to jump more than others.
> The jump-loving fleas become soccer players in the circus. They
> wear a harness and kick a tiny Styrofoam ball into a little soccer net.
> These fleas show off their speed.
>
> The fleas that don't like to jump much pull carriages to show off
> their strength. Hans trains these fleas *not* to jump. When they
> learn to walk, not jump, they're ready for a harness and a carriage.

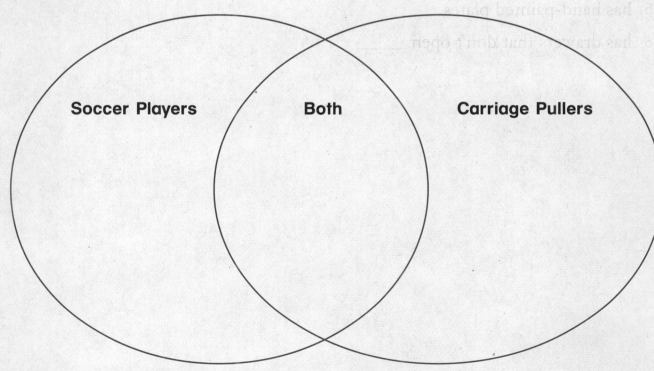

Soccer Players   **Both**   **Carriage Pullers**

Name _____

Remove the Ending

Read each sentence. Write the base word for each underlined word.

> Remember that in the base word
> • a final consonant may have been doubled,
> • a final *e* may have been dropped.

1. One flea <u>crawled</u> into her box. _____

2. She had been <u>practicing</u> her circus act and was tired. _____

3. She had been <u>kicking</u> a tiny soccer ball into a net. _____

4. The flea's harness was <u>bugging</u> her. _____

5. Another flea <u>snored</u> loudly in the box. _____

6. She had been <u>hopping</u> through hoops. _____

7. The first flea <u>cried</u>, "I can hardly wait to lie down!" _____

8. She was already <u>falling</u> asleep. _____

Name _____

Syllable Sounds

**Say each word aloud. Count the number of vowel sounds.
Write the word syllable by syllable, with a dot (•) to separate the
syllables. Then check your word division in a dictionary.**

1. flickering _____

2. daughter _____

3. trembling _____

4. caught _____

5. gingerly _____

6. carousel _____

7. giant _____

8. experience _____

9. enormous _____

10. centimeters _____

syl•la•ble

syl•la•ble

syl•la•ble

Name _____

Spelling Review

Write Spelling Words from the list on this page to answer the questions.

1–10. Which ten words are compound words? They can be written as one word, as hyphenated words, or as two words.

1. _____ 6. _____
2. _____ 7. _____
3. _____ 8. _____
4. _____ 9. _____
5. _____ 10. _____

11–20. Which ten words end with the /ər/, /l/, or /əl/ sounds? Bonus: Put a check mark beside the compound word above that ends with the /ər/ sound.

11. _____ 16. _____
12. _____ 17. _____
13. _____ 18. _____
14. _____ 19. _____
15. _____ 20. _____

21–30. Which ten words end with *-ed* or *-ing*?

21. _____ 26. _____
22. _____ 27. _____
23. _____ 28. _____
24. _____ 29. _____
25. _____ 30. _____

Spelling Words

1. weather
2. doctor
3. airport
4. understand
5. raced
6. smelling
7. anything
8. uncle
9. pleasing
10. ninety-nine
11. fainted
12. beggar
13. seat belt
14. final
15. all right
16. proper
17. battle
18. make-believe
19. towel
20. snapping
21. whenever
22. skipped
23. hiking
24. trouble
25. medal
26. striped
27. homesick
28. railroad
29. dimmed
30. checking

Name _____

Spelling Spree

Book Titles Write the Spelling Word that best completes
each book title. Remember to use capital letters.

1. *Aunt Angela and* _____ *Ed*
   by Watt A. Life

2. *Fasten Your* _____*! Blast Off!*
   by Rock Ottship

3. *Our* _____ *Day in the Jungle*
   by I. M. Lost

4. *Now I* _____: *Science Made
   Simple* by Sy N. Smaster

5. *The Mystery of the* _____
   Without Planes by A. D. Tektiv

6. *The* _____ *Station at the End
   of the Tracks* by Steem N. Jin

7. *Eat Vegetables* _____ *You Like:
   A Guide to Healthy Eating* by Dr. Eetmore Greenes

1. battle
2. airport
3. all right
4. homesick
5. railroad
6. understand
7. anything
8. make-believe
9. whenever
10. trouble
11. ninety-nine
12. seat belt
13. final
14. proper
15. uncle

The Next Word Write the Spelling Word that belongs
with each group of words.

8. seventy-seven, eighty-eight, _____

9. correct, right, fitting, _____

10. nothing, something, _____

11. fight, struggle, war, _____

12. good, okay, _____

13. lonesome, sad, _____

14. fantasy, pretend, _____

15. problem, worry, _____

Name _____

Proofreading and Writing

Proofreading Circle the six misspelled Spelling Words in Professor Mick Stupp's diary of backward adventures. Then write each word correctly.

1. fainted
2. checking
3. beggar
4. towel
5. hiking
6. dimmed
7. weather
8. snapping
9. pleasing
10. doctor
11. medal
12. raced
13. smelling
14. striped
15. skipped

August 32nd At ten this morning it was just getting dark. The wether was fine, but it was raining hard. Now I've seen anything! I met a begger sitting on a towle. I gave him a million-dollar bill, and he faynted. I went hikeing down the street to find him a docter. What a day!

1. _____   4. _____
2. _____   5. _____
3. _____   6. _____

Mixed-up News Use Spelling Words to complete the following paragraph of a TV news report.

Our reporter has been 7. _____ on Professor Stupp's latest adventure. She has not 8. _____ any details. The professor ended up 9. _____ like fish, after he fell into a fish barrel. The mayor awarded him a 10. _____ on a blue-and-white 11. _____ ribbon. The ribbon was 12. _____ to most, but Professor Stupp's smile 13. _____ when he saw it wasn't red! Still, he 14. _____ quickly offstage, 15. _____ his fingers and saying, "Time for adventure!"

✏ **Create an Adventure** On a separate sheet of paper, write about another adventure of Professor Mick Stupp. Use the Spelling Review Words.

Name _____

Identifying Action Verbs

Circle the action verb in each sentence.

1. A family of Borrowers lived beneath the floorboards.

2. Borrowers usually avoid big people.

3. This family's child talked to a huge boy.

4. Her parents worried about that friendship.

5. The huge boy discovered the family's home.

6. He asked the young Borrower a question.

7. She whispered an answer.

8. The boy offered the family a doll's dresser.

9. He opened its cupboard.

10. The tiny family accepted the gift from the boy.

Name _____

Identifying the Tense

Underline the verb in each sentence. Then write whether the verb is in the *present tense*, the *past tense*, or the *future tense*.

1. Lila watched a movie about a tiny family last night. _____

2. She enjoys books about little people, too. _____

3. Her brother teases her about this. _____

4. He will gather some tiny objects tonight. _____

5. Then he will arrange them on Lila's desk. _____

6. Last week he played a different trick on her. _____

7. He printed tiny words on the back of a stamp. _____

8. Lila ignores her brother. _____

9. She will talk with her friends. _____

10. They share her interest in fantasy tales. _____

Student Handbook

Contents

How to Study a Word

1. LOOK at the word.

► What does the word mean?

► What letters are in the word?

► Name and touch each letter.

2. SAY the word.

► Listen for the consonant sounds.

► Listen for the vowel sounds.

3. THINK about the word.

► How is each sound spelled?

► Close your eyes and picture the word.

► What familiar spelling patterns do you see?

► Did you see any prefixes, suffixes, or other word parts?

4. WRITE the word.

► Think about the sounds and the letters.

► Form the letters correctly.

5. CHECK the spelling.

► Did you spell the word the same way it is spelled in your word list?

► If you did not spell the word correctly, write the word again.

again	eighth	January		
all right	enough			
a lot	every	knew		
also	everybody	know	really	two
always	everyone		received	tying
another	excite	let's	right	
anyone		letter		until
anything	family	little	said	usually
anyway	favorite	loose	Saturday	
around	February	lose	school	very
	finally	lying	someone	
beautiful	first		stopped	weird
because	friend	might	stretch	we're
before		millimeter	suppose	where
believe	getting	minute	sure	while
brought	girl	morning	swimming	whole
build	goes	myself		won't
buy	going		than	world
	guess	ninety	that's	would
cannot			their	wouldn't
can't	happened	o'clock	then	write
caught	haven't	off	there	writing
choose	heard	once	there's	
chose	height	other	they	your
clothes	here	our	they're	you're
coming			thought	
could	I'd	people	through	
cousin	I'll	pretty	to	
	I'm	probably	tongue	
didn't	instead		tonight	
different	into	quit	too	
divide	its	quite	tried	
don't	it's		truly	

Grandfather's Journey

The /ĭ/, /ī/, /ŏ/, /ō/ Sounds

/ĭ/ → st**i**ll
/ī/ → cr**ime**, fl**igh**t, gr**i**nd
/ŏ/ → sh**o**ck
/ō/ → wr**ote**, c**oa**st, sn**ow**, g**o**ld

Spelling Words

1. snow
2. grind
3. still
4. coast
5. odd
6. crime
7. gold
8. wrote
9. flight
10. build
11. broke
12. blind
13. folk
14. grown
15. shock
16. ripe
17. coal
18. inch
19. sigh
20. built

Challenge Words

1. remind
2. approach
3. rigid
4. recognize
5. continent

My Study List
Add your own spelling words on the back. ➡

Journeys
Reading-Writing Workshop

Look for familiar spelling patterns in these words to help you remember their spellings.

Spelling Words

1. cannot
2. can't
3. don't
4. haven't
5. won't
6. wouldn't
7. I'd
8. I'll
9. let's
10. we're
11. I'm
12. didn't
13. o'clock
14. that's
15. there's

Challenge Words

1. minute
2. stretch
3. instead
4. ninety
5. divide

My Study List
Add your own spelling words on the back. ➡

Akiak

The /ă/, /ā/, /ĕ/, and /ē/ Sounds

/ă/ → p**a**st
/ā/ → s**afe**, g**ai**n, gr**ay**
/ĕ/ → k**e**pt
/ē/ → r**ea**ch, sw**ee**t

Spelling Words

1. gain
2. cream
3. sweet
4. safe
5. past
6. reach
7. kept
8. gray
9. field
10. break
11. east
12. shape
13. steep
14. pray
15. pain
16. glass
17. west
18. cheap
19. steak
20. chief

Challenge Words

1. graceful
2. descent
3. athletic
4. knead
5. activity

My Study List
Add your own spelling words on the back. ➡

Take-Home Word List

Take-Home Word List

Name _____

My Study List

1. _____
2. _____
3. _____
4. _____
5. _____
6. _____
7. _____
8. _____
9. _____
10. _____

Review Words

1. need
2. last
3. stage
4. left
5. paint

How to Study a Word

Look at the word.
Say the word.
Think about the word.
Write the word.
Check the spelling.

Take-Home Word List

Name _____

My Study List

1. _____
2. _____
3. _____
4. _____
5. _____
6. _____
7. _____
8. _____
9. _____
10. _____

How to Study a Word

Look at the word.
Say the word.
Think about the word.
Write the word.
Check the spelling.

Take-Home Word List

Name _____

My Study List

1. _____
2. _____
3. _____
4. _____
5. _____
6. _____
7. _____
8. _____
9. _____
10. _____

Review Words

1. drop
2. mix
3. smoke
4. sight
5. know

How to Study a Word

Look at the word.
Say the word.
Think about the word.
Write the word.
Check the spelling.

Journeys
Spelling Review

Spelling Words

1. safe	16. few
2. kept	17. trunk
3. gray	18. steal
4. grown	19. weight
5. wrote	20. meat
6. blind	21. past
7. suit	22. reach
8. crumb	23. coast
9. wait	24. odd
10. creak	25. sigh
11. steep	26. true
12. gain	27. tube
13. still	28. steel
14. gold	29. creek
15. crime	30. meet

See the back for
Challenge Words.

By the Shores of
Silver Lake

Homophones
Homophones are words
that sound alike but have
different spellings and
meanings.

Spelling Words

1. steel	11. beet
2. steal	12. beat
3. lead	13. meet
4. led	14. meat
5. wait	15. peek
6. weight	16. peak
7. wear	17. deer
8. ware	18. dear
9. creak	19. ring
10. creek	20. wring

Challenge Words

1. pour
2. pore
3. vain
4. vein
5. vane

Finding the *Titanic*

**The /ŭ/, /yo͞o/, and
/o͞o/ Sounds**

/ŭ/	➡	brush
/yo͞o/	➡	tube, few,
and /o͞o/		true, juice

Spelling Words

1. brush	11. suit
2. juice	12. pump
3. fruit	13. due
4. tube	14. dull
5. lunch	15. tune
6. crumb	16. blew
7. few	17. trunk
8. true	18. sum
9. truth	19. glue
10. done	20. threw

Challenge Words

1. newscast
2. commute
3. continue
4. attitude
5. slumber

My Study List
Add your own
spelling words
on the back. ➡

My Study List
Add your own
spelling words
on the back. ➡

My Study List
Add your own
spelling words
on the back. ➡

Take-Home Word List

Take-Home Word List

My Study List

1. _____
2. _____
3. _____
4. _____
5. _____
6. _____
7. _____
8. _____
9. _____
10. _____

Review Words

1. chew
2. blue
3. rub
4. shut
5. June

How to Study a Word

Look at the word.
Say the word.
Think about the word.
Write the word.
Check the spelling.

Take-Home Word List

My Study List

1. _____
2. _____
3. _____
4. _____
5. _____
6. _____
7. _____
8. _____
9. _____
10. _____

Review Words

1. its
2. it's
3. there
4. their
5. they're

How to Study a Word

Look at the word.
Say the word.
Think about the word.
Write the word.
Check the spelling.

Take-Home Word List

My Study List

1. _____
2. _____
3. _____
4. _____
5. _____
6. _____
7. _____
8. _____
9. _____
10. _____

Challenge Words

1. descent
2. graceful
3. rigid
4. newscast
5. knead
6. remind
7. continue
8. pour
9. slumber
10. pore

How to Study a Word

Look at the word.
Say the word.
Think about the word.
Write the word.
Check the spelling.

Tanya's Reunion

The /o͞o/ and /o͝o/ Sounds

/o͞o/ → t**oo**l
/o͝o/ → w**oo**d, p**u**t

Spelling Words

1. wood
2. brook
3. tool
4. put
5. wool
6. push
7. full
8. roof
9. group
10. prove
11. stood
12. stool
13. hook
14. smooth
15. shoot
16. bush
17. fool
18. pull
19. soup
20. move

Challenge Words

1. soot
2. marooned
3. pudding
4. cocoon
5. superb

My Study List
Add your own spelling words on the back. ➡

American Stories
Reading-Writing Workshop

Look for familiar spelling patterns in these words to help you remember their spellings.

Spelling Words

1. a lot
2. other
3. another
4. anyone
5. every
6. someone
7. myself
8. family
9. friend
10. people
11. again
12. anything
13. anyway
14. everyone
15. first

Challenge Words

1. beautiful
2. clothes
3. cousin
4. everybody
5. weird

My Study List
Add your own spelling words on the back. ➡

Tomás and the Library Lady

The /ou/ and /ô/ Sounds

/ou/ → h**ow**l, p**ou**nd
/ô/ → j**aw**, c**au**se, **a**lways

Spelling Words

1. pound
2. howl
3. jaw
4. bounce
5. cause
6. always
7. shout
8. aloud
9. south
10. couple
11. drawn
12. scout
13. false
14. proud
15. frown
16. sauce
17. gown
18. couch
19. dawn
20. mount

Challenge Words

1. gnaw
2. prowl
3. pounce
4. doubt
5. scrawny

My Study List
Add your own spelling words on the back. ➡

Take-Home Word List

Take-Home Word List

Take-Home Word List

Name _____

My Study List

1. _____
2. _____
3. _____
4. _____
5. _____
6. _____
7. _____
8. _____
9. _____
10. _____

Review Words

1. walk
2. lawn
3. loud
4. sound
5. clown

How to Study a Word

Look at the word.
Say the word.
Think about the word.
Write the word.
Check the spelling.

286

Name _____

My Study List

1. _____
2. _____
3. _____
4. _____
5. _____
6. _____
7. _____
8. _____
9. _____
10. _____

How to Study a Word

Look at the word.
Say the word.
Think about the word.
Write the word.
Check the spelling.

286

Name _____

My Study List

1. _____
2. _____
3. _____
4. _____
5. _____
6. _____
7. _____
8. _____
9. _____
10. _____

Review Words

1. cook
2. spoon
3. shook
4. school
5. tooth

How to Study a Word

Look at the word.
Say the word.
Think about the word.
Write the word.
Check the spelling.

286

American Stories
Spelling Review

Spelling Words

1. howl
2. false
3. sauce
4. put
5. roof
6. hardly
7. dairy
8. charge
9. dirty
10. world
11. bounce
12. couch
13. wood
14. push
15. pull
16. year
17. alarm
18. horse
19. curl
20. return
21. jaw
22. dawn
23. tool
24. full
25. gear
26. spare
27. cheer
28. chore
29. heard
30. search

**See the back for
Challenge Words.**

My Study List
Add your own
spelling words
on the back. ➡

A Very Important Day

**The /ôr/, /ûr/, and
/yŏŏr/ Sounds**

/ôr/	➡	horse, chore
/ûr/	➡	firm, curve, learn, worm
/yŏŏr/	➡	pure

Spelling Words

1. horse
2. chore
3. firm
4. learn
5. dirty
6. curve
7. world
8. pure
9. board
10. course
11. heard
12. return
13. cure
14. score
15. worm
16. thirteen
17. worn
18. curl
19. shirt
20. search

Challenge Words

1. thoroughbred
2. fortunate
3. hurdle
4. foreign
5. earnest

My Study List
Add your own
spelling words
on the back. ➡

Boss of the Plains

**The /îr/, /är/, and
/âr/ Sounds**

/îr/	➡	gear, cheer
/är/	➡	sharp
/âr/	➡	stare, hairy

Spelling Words

1. gear
2. spear
3. sharp
4. stare
5. alarm
6. cheer
7. square
8. hairy
9. heart
10. weird
11. starve
12. charm
13. beard
14. hardly
15. spare
16. stairs
17. year
18. charge
19. dairy
20. scarce

Challenge Words

1. pioneer
2. awareness
3. startle
4. marvel
5. weary

My Study List
Add your own
spelling words
on the back. ➡

Name _____

My Study List

1. _____
2. _____
3. _____
4. _____
5. _____
6. _____
7. _____
8. _____
9. _____
10. _____

Review Words

1. air
2. near
3. large
4. scare
5. chair

How to Study a Word

Look at the word.
Say the word.
Think about the word.
Write the word.
Check the spelling.

288

Name _____

My Study List

1. _____
2. _____
3. _____
4. _____
5. _____
6. _____
7. _____
8. _____
9. _____
10. _____

Review Words

1. first
2. hurt
3. work
4. third
5. storm

How to Study a Word

Look at the word.
Say the word.
Think about the word.
Write the word.
Check the spelling.

288

Name _____

My Study List

1. _____
2. _____
3. _____
4. _____
5. _____
6. _____
7. _____
8. _____
9. _____
10. _____

Challenge Words

1. pounce	6. scrawny
2. pudding	7. marooned
3. cocoon	8. pioneer
4. awareness	9. marvel
5. fortunate	10. earnest

How to Study a Word

Look at the word.
Say the word.
Think about the word.
Write the word.
Check the spelling.

288

Cendrillon

> **Final /ər/, /l/, or /əl/**
>
> /ər/ → weath**er**, harb**or**, sug**ar**
>
> /l/ → mod**el**, fin**al**,
>
> or /əl/ → midd**le**

Spelling Words

1. harbor
2. final
3. middle
4. weather
5. labor
6. model
7. chapter
8. special
9. sugar
10. bottle
11. medal
12. collar
13. proper
14. towel
15. beggar
16. battle
17. trouble
18. shower
19. uncle
20. doctor

Challenge Words

1. shoulder
2. decimal
3. trifle
4. solar
5. cancel

My Study List
Add your own spelling words on the back. ➡

That's Amazing!
Reading-Writing Workshop

Look for familiar spelling patterns in these words to help you remember their spellings.

Spelling Words

1. tonight
2. whole
3. while
4. could
5. world
6. writing
7. build
8. school
9. finished
10. morning
11. coming
12. stopped
13. getting
14. goes
15. going

Challenge Words

1. happened
2. received
3. believe
4. quit
5. quite

My Study List
Add your own spelling words on the back. ➡

The Stranger

> **Compound Words**
> A compound word may be written as one word, as two words joined by a hyphen, or as two separate words.

Spelling Words

1. railroad
2. airport
3. seat belt
4. everywhere
5. homesick
6. understand
7. background
8. anything
9. ninety-nine
10. already
11. fireplace
12. ourselves
13. all right
14. forever
15. breakfast
16. whenever
17. everything
18. meanwhile
19. afternoon
20. make-believe

Challenge Words

1. landmark
2. nationwide
3. postscript
4. motorcycle
5. handkerchief

My Study List
Add your own spelling words on the back. ➡

Name _____

My Study List

1. _____
2. _____
3. _____
4. _____
5. _____
6. _____
7. _____
8. _____
9. _____
10. _____

Review Words

1. inside
2. outside
3. birthday
4. baseball
5. sometimes

How to Study a Word

Look at the word.
Say the word.
Think about the word.
Write the word.
Check the spelling.

290

Name _____

My Study List

1. _____
2. _____
3. _____
4. _____
5. _____
6. _____
7. _____
8. _____
9. _____
10. _____

How to Study a Word

Look at the word.
Say the word.
Think about the word.
Write the word.
Check the spelling.

290

Name _____

My Study List

1. _____
2. _____
3. _____
4. _____
5. _____
6. _____
7. _____
8. _____
9. _____
10. _____

Review Words

1. neighbor
2. little
3. dollar
4. daughter
5. circle

How to Study a Word

Look at the word.
Say the word.
Think about the word.
Write the word.
Check the spelling.

290

That's Amazing!
Spelling Review

Spelling Words

1. railroad
2. homesick
3. anything
4. seat belt
5. battle
6. beggar
7. doctor
8. smelling
9. pleasing
10. dimmed
11. airport
12. understand
13. ninety-nine
14. final
15. trouble
16. towel
17. medal
18. striped
19. skipped
20. checking
21. all right
22. make-believe
23. whenever
24. proper
25. uncle
26. weather
27. raced
28. snapping
29. hiking
30. fainted

See the back for Challenge Words.

Heat Wave!

> ### Words with -ed or -ing
> race + **ed** = rac**ed**
> land + **ed** = land**ed**
> snap + **ing** = sna**pping**

Spelling Words

1. dancing
2. skipped
3. hiking
4. flipped
5. snapping
6. raced
7. landed
8. pleasing
9. checking
10. dared
11. dimmed
12. rubbing
13. striped
14. wasting
15. traced
16. stripped
17. tanning
18. smelling
19. phoning
20. fainted

Challenge Words

1. breathing
2. tiring
3. urged
4. scrubbed
5. striving

My Study List
Add your own spelling words on the back. ➡

My Study List
Add your own spelling words on the back. ➡

Name _____

My Study List

1. _____
2. _____
3. _____
4. _____
5. _____
6. _____
7. _____
8. _____
9. _____
10. _____

Review Words

1. cared
2. joking
3. tapping
4. wrapped
5. fixing

How to Study a Word

Look at the word.
Say the word.
Think about the word.
Write the word.
Check the spelling.

Name _____

My Study List

1. _____
2. _____
3. _____
4. _____
5. _____
6. _____
7. _____
8. _____
9. _____
10. _____

Challenge Words

1. handkerchief   6. postscript
2. motorcycle   7. shoulder
3. decimal   8. cancel
4. scrubbed   9. breathing
5. striving   10. urged

How to Study a Word

Look at the word.
Say the word.
Think about the word.
Write the word.
Check the spelling.

Focus on Plays

More Homophones
Homophones are words that sound alike but have different spellings and meanings.

Spelling Words

1. heard	11. heal
2. herd	12. heel
3. loan	13. steak
4. lone	14. stake
5. flea	15. pare
6. flee	16. pear
7. hall	17. berry
8. haul	18. bury
9. forth	19. groan
10. fourth	20. grown

Challenge Words

1. cereal
2. serial
3. ceiling
4. sealing

My Study List
Add your own spelling words on the back. ➡

Focus on Mysteries

More Short and Long Vowels

short vowel sounds ➡	plant, desk, fist, block, truck
/ā/ ➡	shake, spray, drain
/ē/ ➡	neat, speed
/ī/ ➡	fright, pride
/ō/ ➡	roast, cone
/ū/ ➡	prune, crew

Spelling Words

1. shake	11. speed
2. desk	12. drain
3. block	13. fist
4. fright	14. pride
5. neat	15. truck
6. roast	16. flock
7. prune	17. cone
8. spray	18. crew
9. plant	19. blade
10. bread	20. dead

Challenge Words

1. proceed	4. erase
2. cocoa	5. polish
3. imitate	

My Study List
Add your own spelling words on the back. ➡

Name _____

My Study List

1. _____
2. _____
3. _____
4. _____
5. _____
6. _____
7. _____
8. _____
9. _____
10. _____

Review Words

1. drum
2. street
3. flew
4. bright
5. float

How to Study a Word

Look at the word.
Say the word.
Think about the word.
Write the word.
Check the spelling.

294

Name _____

My Study List

1. _____
2. _____
3. _____
4. _____
5. _____
6. _____
7. _____
8. _____
9. _____
10. _____

Review Words

1. bare
2. bear
3. plane
4. plain

How to Study a Word

Look at the word.
Say the word.
Think about the word.
Write the word.
Check the spelling.

294

Problem Words

Words	Rules	Examples
are our	*Are* is a verb. *Our* is a possessive pronoun.	<u>Are</u> these gloves yours? This is <u>our</u> car.
doesn't don't	Use *doesn't* with singular nouns, *he*, *she*, and *it*. Use *don't* with plural nouns, *I*, *you*, *we*, and *they*.	Dad <u>doesn't</u> swim. We <u>don't</u> swim.
good well	Use the adjective *good* to describe nouns. Use the adverb *well* to describe verbs.	The weather looks <u>good</u>. She sings <u>well</u>.
its it's	*Its* is a possessive pronoun. *It's* is a contraction of *it is*.	The dog wagged <u>its</u> tail. <u>It's</u> cold today.
set sit	*Set* means "to put." *Sit* means "to rest or stay in one place."	<u>Set</u> the vase on the table. Please <u>sit</u> in this chair.
their there they're	*Their* means "belonging to them." *There* means "at or in that place." *They're* is a contraction of *they are*.	<u>Their</u> coats are on the bed. Is Carlos <u>there</u>? <u>They're</u> going to the store.
two to too	*Two* is a number *To* means "toward." *Too* means "also" or "more than enough."	I bought <u>two</u> shirts. A cat ran <u>to</u> the tree. Can we go <u>too</u>? I ate <u>too</u> many peas.
your you're	*Your* is a possessive pronoun. *You're* is a contraction of *you are*.	Are these <u>your</u> glasses? <u>You're</u> late again!

Read each question below. Then check your paper. Correct any mistakes you find. After you have corrected them, put a check mark in the box next to the question.

☐ 1. Did I indent each paragraph?

☐ 2. Does each sentence tell one complete thought?

☐ 3. Do I have any run-on sentences?

☐ 4. Did I spell all words correctly?

☐ 5. Did I use capital letters correctly?

☐ 6. Did I use punctuation marks correctly?

☐ 7. Did I use commas and apostrophes correctly?

☐ 8. Did I spell all the words the right way?

Is there anything else you should look for? Make your own proofreading checklist.

☐ _____

☐ _____

☐ _____

☐ _____

☐ _____

☐ _____

☐ _____

Mark	Explanation	Examples
¶	Begin a new paragraph. Indent the paragraph.	¶The boat finally arrived. It was two hours late.
∧	Add letters, words, or sentences.	My best friend ate lunch with me today.
୨	Take out words, sentences, and punctuation marks. Correct spelling.	We looked at and admired the moddel airplanes.
≡	Change a small letter to a capital letter.	New York city is exciting.
/	Change a capital letter to a small letter.	The Fireflies blinked in the dark.
ⱽ ⱽ	Add quotation marks.	Where do you want the piano? asked the movers.
∧	Add a comma.	Carlton my cat has a mind of his own.
⊙	Add a period.	Put a period at the end of the sentence
∼	Reverse letters or words.	Raed carefully the instructions
?	Add a question mark.	Should I put the mark here
!	Add an exclamation mark.	Look out below